Monitor Messages

Biblical Monitor Messages
On Many Subjects

Vernon Long

All scripture verses are from the
KJV Translation

This book was printed in the United States of America.
Cover design by Matthew Long

To order additional copies of this book, contact:

Vernon Long
P. O. Box 1514
Desloge, Missouri 63601

FWB Publications
Columbus, Ohio

FWB

Preface

The internet ministry of *'Monitor Messages'* began when a North Carolina pastor lost all of the messages he had received from Vernon Long and asked if he would replace them. The replacement messages were sent on a CD and this was the first *'Monitor Messages'* CD produced and the messages in this book are on the first CD. The CD contains manuscripts of 368 messages. This first CD of *'Monitor Messages'* is FREE to all who purchase this book. Subsequently there have been seven other CDs produced on other messages that have been previously preached on various subjects, as listed on the order blank for the FREE CD.

Webster defines *monitor* as: one that warns or instructs; one that monitors or is used in monitoring: also as a cathode-ray tube used for display (as of television pictures or computer information). One usually thinks of a monitor as a display screen which these messages are shown on. The intent of all the CDs produced is that the Scriptures, with the Holy Spirit's help will use them *'as one that warns or instructs; one that monitors or is used in monitoring.'*

My Tribute To My Wife

Ada was a **faithful wife** for 59 years. She was always there when I needed her.

We had a great marriage and the few disagreements we had were over minor issues. She was always willing to forgive when I asked for her forgiveness and I failed to be the husband I should have been. ***Proverbs 18:22, whoso findeth a wife findeth a good thing, and obtaineth favour of the LORD.*** Much of the favor I obtained from the Lord was due to the good wife I found, even before we both became Christians. Ada was definitely *'a prudent wife' (Proverbs 19:14)*, understanding things, that at times were hard for me to understand.

Ada was a **faithful mother**. When I was running from the Lord's calling into the ministry, working three jobs, and not at home that much, she did what I should have been doing—***bringing our children up in the nurture and admonition of the Lord, Ephesians 6:4***. She did a good job, as our two living children, Sheila and Matthew, are serving the Lord. Our oldest daughter Cindy (now deceased), who had strayed from the Lord, came back to Him and was more involved in the youth ministry than we ever knew. Her pastor mentioned this during her funeral message. I know the results of our children being what they became was a result of a mother's prayers.

All glory goes to the Lord, but in our family altar time, with our children participating, we did our best to ***train up a child in the way he should go: and when he is old, he will not depart from it, Proverbs 22:6.***

I have many *'precious memories'* of our family altar times. Ada definitely loved her children. ***Beloved in the sight of my mother, Proverbs 4:3.*** She really loved her grandchildren and great grandchildren.

Ada was a **faithful pastor's wife.** Many judge a pastor's wife by the talents they have, i.e., singing, playing the piano, etc. I want no one to think that I am not thankful for pastor's wives that have such talents, but the qualities that Ada had in her life as a pastor's wife outweighs any talents she could have had. I was a deacon before I answered the call to preach and she definitely met all the qualifications of a deacon's wife as given in ***1 Timothy 3:11, Even so must their wives be grave, not slanderers, sober, faithful in all things.***

I could say much more about Ada being a faithful wife, a faithful mother, and a faithful pastor's wife. I can say that she was **faithful in all things**, besides being a faithful wife, mother, and pastor's wife. She will be missed, not only by those of our family, but also by the many friends she had over the years. *Revelation 14:13, And I heard a voice from heaven saying unto me, Write, Blessed are the dead which die in the Lord from henceforth: Yea, saith the Spirit, that they may rest from their labours; and their works do follow them.*

In Memory of Mammaw Ada Long
Michelle (Haas) Forlines

A very special little lady died last week. My Mammaw. Growing up we didn't get to see my Mammaw and Pappaw very often. Maybe once a year. After becoming an adult and moving to Tennessee is when I began spending more time with them. Mammaw was crippled from Rheumatoid arthritis my whole life. I remember when she walked on her own and how she would wring out the dishcloth by pushing it on the side of the sink. As a child I was fascinated by her crooked toes and fingers. Since I've known her she's gotten progressively shorter and more crippled over the years. As much as her crippled body held her back, she loved life and did as much as she could by herself. When she could no longer cook by herself, she would let Pappaw know exactly what

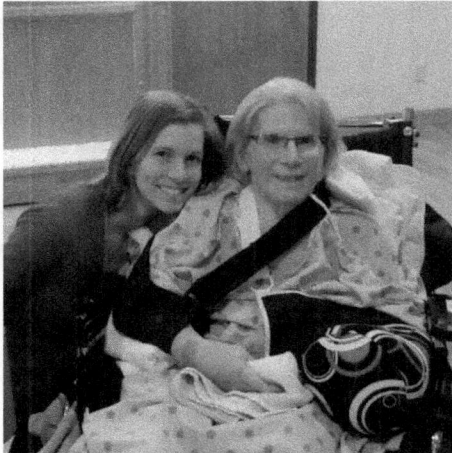

she wanted to eat. And man was she a picky eater! She had a dry wit that matched Pappaw's silly boisterous humor. She always cried when we would leave after a visit. Her prayers were quiet and fervent and usually tearful. She would get on to Pappaw in her scratchy little voice for eating too much and for spending too much time on the computer. But they loved each other and still slept in the same bed even after Pappaw gave her a black eye one night. He is a loud and active dreamer. Mammaw always said that's how she found out what Pappaw was thinking about. She'd listen to him talk and preach and yell in his sleep. She said that when he got too rowdy she'd just scootch to the edge of the bed to get away from him. Some of my sweetest memories with Mammaw are from 2010 when I went to stay with them for about 3 weeks after she had a fall. We talked a lot about her life and her memories. I'm thankful for Mammaw's life. I'm thankful for Pappaw and how he cared for her so many years. I'm thankful for the friends that live near them that have cared for and loved them so well. I'm going to miss my Mammaw.

A Tribute to Cindy from Her Church

Milldale Presbyterian Church

Springfield, Tennessee

On December 13th we celebrated the life of our friend and sister in Christ Cindy Craig. We were able have a special dinner for Cindy's family at the church. It was such a blessing getting to know them -Pastor Vernon & Ada Long (Cindy's parents), Matt & Melony Long (her brother & sister-in-law), Sheila & Pastor Melvin Haas (her sister & brother-in-law), along with many other family members. We now have a better understanding why Cindy was so very special.

Cindy's impact on our church is impossible to set in words. Her many contributions to our lives have been profound. Her smile and joy was infectious. Her authenticity helped us to look at ourselves more honestly. Our continued condolences go out to Cody, Darcie and family. We pray that their grief might be eased by the love and consolation of the body of Christ. On December 21st the children led us in worship through a program that Cindy wrote. Diane Campbell stepped up to lead our children and it was wonderful. Cindy's brother Matt played Cindy's puppet "Izzy the Poet" and his wife Melony helped out also. They came from Indiana and we are so grateful. Cindy's Christmas Program was so emotional and very touching, a special tribute to her.

She is still deeply missed and we pray that in the days and months to come we will adjust to her absence... resting in the hope that to be "absent in the body is to be present with the Lord."

Table of Contents

Section One: Messages

Section Two: Fact Sheets

Section Three: Cantata

Section Four: Order information

Section One
Messages

Autobiography of a Faulty Foundation

Matt.7:21-27

21 Not everyone that saith unto me, Lord, Lord, shall enter into the kingdom of heaven; but he that doeth the will of my Father which is in heaven.

22 Many will say to me in that day, Lord, Lord, have we not prophesied in thy name? And in thy name have we not cast out devils? And in thy name done many wonderful works?

23 And then will I profess unto them, I never knew you: depart from me, ye that work iniquity.

24 Therefore whosoever heareth these sayings of mine, and doeth them, I will liken him unto a wise man, which built his house upon a rock:

25 And the rain descended, and the floods came, and the winds blew, and beat upon that house; and it fell not: for it was founded upon a rock.

26 And every one that heareth these sayings of mine, and doeth them not, shall be likened unto a foolish man, which built his house upon the sand:

27 And the rain descended, and the floods came, and the winds blew, and beat upon that house; and it fell: and great was the fall of it.

This message is a personal testimony of my life and how I tried to build my life on some *faulty foundations*. I will give a sketchy biography of my life. This is not a *'tell all'* of all the sins in my life, but primarily is about my rebellion against God's will for my life. There are a lot of 'I's' and 'mys' used, but 'I' am nothing without Christ.

The first event of my life was conception, some 9 months before **April 15, 1935**. I was a depression baby, the 6th and last child of my parents, **John and Myrtle Long**. My parents were poor, as a lot of people were in those days, and they were already feeding 5 hungry mouths besides themselves. Mom said she cried when she told Dad she was with child, and they were not tears of joy, as *'I was not planned for'*. That is the way they said it back then; today people call it an *'unwanted pregnancy,'* and many little babies are killed before they are born. The Bible teaches that I was a living person before I was born into this world *(Psa.139:13-16)*. God had a plan and purpose for my life, as He had for Jeremiah and everyone here—*Jer 1:5, Before I formed thee in the belly I knew thee; and before thou camest forth out of the womb I sanctified thee, and I ordained thee a prophet unto the nations*.

Early in my life we moved from Flat River (now Park Hills) MO to a farm on Goose Creek in Bollinger County, near Patton, MO. God spoke to me many times in my childhood, but I refused to hear His voice; Samuel heard His voice as a child *(1 Sam.3:1-10)*. I believe in child evangelism, as I know from personal experience what heartaches and scars that sin can bring in one's life when they continue to resist, even as a child. The Lord continued to speak to me, not only through the preached and taught Word, but by my experience of being raised in a Christian home, [a preacher's home] as well.

I am not too fond of people who tell all about their sinful lifestyle of the past, and hang out their sins for all to see. I feel that sometimes it can be taken wrong and young people think they can get by with sinning, and later repent and everything will be O.K. I will not tell you about all my sins, but I will tell you that I lived sinful during my high school years—drinking, smoking, using profanity, and other sins that were against all I had been taught in a Christian home. If I would have died as a teenager, I would be burning in hell today, that is the message teenagers and young people need to hear about my sinful past. I am so thankful for the prayers of my mom and dad for me, and thankful for a *'longsuffering God, not willing that I should perish, but should come to repentance' 2 Pet 3:9*.

My sophomore year in high school I made the 'A' basketball team, which made me popular, but *popularity does not bring happiness*! Earlier in my life I had run into a barbed wire fence, which could have killed me. My parents were concerned about the injury on my neck and the scar tissue from a previous surgery, so I had a skin graft operation from my leg to my neck the first part of my junior year in high school, and the Lord took away my ability in playing basketball, which I never did regain. I almost became a drop-out my Senior year, as I had worked in St. Louis that summer, and dad was called to pastor Parkview Free Will Baptist Church in Desloge, MO and I didn't care about going my Senior year to Desloge High School. I went back to school at Patton a month late and caught up in my studies, and stayed with my sister, Geraldine, the first half of the school year, then got a job at Whitener's store and stayed with them.

After graduation from high school I worked for a while driving a cattle and feed truck for Whitener and Wallace stores, in Patton and Marble Hill, MO; then I worked in St. Louis at Wagner Electric, and was still living in sin. I roomed in a boarding home with an alcoholic and was well on my way to the gutter of sin, when God intervened. How did He intervene? **I was laid off in the recession of 1954—*by God's sovereignty and grace*!**

I came back home to Desloge, MO, where my dad was still pastoring the Parkview Free Will Baptist Church and worked at several jobs in the area, and ended up with one of the better jobs in the area, driving a delivery truck for Leadbelt Cleaners.

The latter part of 1954 something happened to me that had not happened before, I met my future wife Ada at the Busy Bee Restaurant, where she worked as a car hop. I started dating her, and even though she was not saved, as myself, she had higher morals than I did. I pretty soon decided this was the girl I wanted to live with for the rest of my life, and we were married on **Feb. 11, 1956**. God knew my future, even though I continued to resist and rebel against Him. Through His foreknowledge

He knew that I would need a wife like Ada, when I surrendered my life to the ministry. What is an ideal pastor's wife? There are various opinions about that, as stated in the *'Tribute to Ada'* that I wrote, and I believe I had one of the best!

October, 1956, I started working at Dow Chemical, one of twelve original operators they trained before the plant started operating, and worked there for the next 17½ years. I had now found a good paying job, which offered good benefits and security. I worked my way up to shift leader, and then later after I had made a decision to live for the Lord, which I will relate later, I bid on the lab job, so I could be off on Sundays to do my duties at church.

But going back to March, 1957, my dad was still pastoring the church in Desloge, and **Bro. Milton Hollifield** from North Carolina came for a revival. We were attending church there, but due to the shift work and working on Sundays, we were not regular attenders. The revival was when my shift schedule was where we could be attending the services, but you know what we did, we stayed at home. However, my dad and mom had still not given up on us and were praying for us to be saved in that revival, so they came to our apartment, up over Ropers Store in Flat River, and witnessed to us. We both made a profession of faith, but there was something different about my profession than Ada's profession of faith, because I really didn't surrender to Jesus as the Lord of my life; I wanted Him as Savior, but not as my Lord.

On May 18, 1957, my dad baptized me and Ada in the Esther Creek, but I was still rebelling against God's will for my life. Baptism will not wash away rebellion, or any other sin, only the blood of Christ can do that when our sins are confessed and repented of. You know what the Bible says about rebellion and stubbornness? *1 Sam 15:23, For rebellion is as the sin of witchcraft, and stubbornness is as iniquity and idolatry.* An insincere profession, even to the point of baptism, was a *faulty foundation* of my life.

January 15, 1958, a big event happened in my [our] lives. I became a daddy! **Our first child Cindy was born.** She was born with a growth over her spinal column, which was first diagnosed as spina bifida, a congenital defect characterized by imperfect closure of part of the spinal column, exposing some of the nervous system and often resulting in hydrocephalus [water head], paralysis, etc. We took her to St. Louis Children's Hospital; we prayed and were really concerned. It turned out that it was not spina bifida, but the growth was caused by a pinched nerve during her development. God answered our prayers, but I continued to rebel against God's will for my life. We lost Cindy in a fatal car accident on December 10, 2008 and she had come back to the Lord after straying from the Lord and is in heaven today with her mother Ada. We claimed *Prov 22:6, Train up a child in the way he should go: and when he is old, he will not depart from it.* We had moved to Herculaneum, so I would be closer to my job at Dow and we started attending the Free Will Baptist mission in Crystal City, where **Bro. Frank Giunta** pastored. He left to attend Free Will Baptist Bible College in Nashville, TN that summer. I knew that was what I should be doing, but I didn't want to give up a good job to do what God was calling me to do. We bought a house in Festus

April 30, 1960. I was ordained as a deacon in the church at Crystal City. I also served as Sunday School Supt., Adult Sunday School teacher, involved in evangelism, and did the printing for the church. I thought surely God would be satisfied if I was faithful and served Him in a local church, but I was still fighting the call of God into the ministry. I started promoting Gospel singings in our church, which was now in Festus, and thought I could serve God in this way. But it was a *faulty foundation*.

November 18, 1960, another big event happened in our lives. **Our second child Sheila was born.** She also had some health complications with asthma, and again we called upon the Lord for healing and she came through it and was not bothered that much in her childhood and does not have problems with it today. God was using all these circumstances to speak to my heart, but I still refused to answer His call on my life.

January, 1962, I started a radio program in Festus, which developed into a program on Saturday and three programs on Sunday, but I later dropped the Saturday program for other obligations in a business I later started. I worked at the radio station as a Gospel DJ up until June of 1973, and while I was in Bible College working as a DJ at WWGM. I continued to send special holiday programs for a couple of years from

Nashville. While I was at the radio station in Festus I started promoting professional singers, such as the Stamps Quartet, the Oak Ridge Boys, and others. I was disappointed to find out that some of the professional singers didn't know the Lord and believe the Gospel they were singing about. But who was I to judge, for I was no better than they were, as I was rebelling against God, which is *'as the sin of witchcraft,'* as I pointed out earlier. I did stop promoting professional singers and just promoted local Gospel singers that I knew.

July, 1962, I was elected to the St. Louis Executive Board of the Quarterly Conference. I was active in our church's ministry and had attended the conferences regularly. I served on the executive board until I answered the call to preach the Gospel. There was something else that happened in July of 1962. A home missionary from Nova Scotia, Canada, held a service in our church, and stayed in our home. He somehow discerned God's call on my life. I admitted to him that God was speaking to me about preaching His Word, but I still did not let Ada know, or others know that I was fighting God's call to the ministry. Our family visited the mission work in Nova Scotia in 1966 and I intended to surrender to the Lord's will while we were there, but I didn't. Since then the missionary has left the ministry and I heard he had left his wife and family.

July, 1963, one of our full-time evangelists held a city-wide revival in St. Louis and had been in revival with us in Festus the previous summer, after the home missionary had confronted me about my calling to the ministry. I had every intention of talking with the evangelist about it, as he stayed in our home during the revival in our church, but I didn't. However, I did talk with him when he was in the city-wide revival in St. Louis, and he encouraged me to surrender to the Lord's will for my life. This evangelist has also left the ministry and divorced from his wife.

There were some problems in our church at Festus, and my being a deacon put me in a position where I was involved. It nearly brought about complete mental anguish to me when some of the things happened in our church. Bro. Warren Livingston was one of the other deacons serving, and it was while they were at the Festus church that we developed our close friendship with **Warren and Ann Livingston**. Bro. Warren and I stood for what was right, but I have often wondered that perhaps I was the Achan, the sin in the camp, that may have been the cause of God allowing some of the things to happen in our church that He did. God was really dealing with me at that time.

In December of 1964, guess what happened? We finally had a son, as Matthew was born on December 18. He also had some physical complications and had a double hernia operation when he was only a few weeks old. Again we prayed and God answered. The only problem with my prayers, is that they were based on a temporal faith, of getting what I wanted without my trusting faith of surrendering to the Lord.

In 1969 I started a new water pollution control business, while still working at Dow Chemical. I invented and received a patent on a home wastewater treatment plant, selling several of the units. The business was primarily a service business and grew in four years to $34,000, this was in addition to that, I was making ten to eleven thousand dollars a year at Dow. This was a lot of money back in 1969—it's still a lot of money! But I found out that money doesn't satisfy when one is rebelling against the Lord. I was helping our pastor, **Bro. A. B. Brown,** complete his seminary training, as he helped in the business. I thought surely God was using me in this way to help others in the ministry, but it was another *faulty foundation* I was building my life on. Even after I signed the business over to Bro. Dale McCurry, God still used the business to help others, as he sent money to Bro. Dallas Henderson to help with his college expenses.

March, 1973, I started something else —Skyway Tours--a tour company. I was a co-host, with Bro. Raymond Riggs, of a tour to Israel with our pastor and his wife, as well as me and Ada, my brother John Paul and his wife, Pastor Glen Rehkop, and others in our group. God really dealt with me when we had the Lord's Supper near the traditional site of the Garden Tomb, where Christ rose from the dead. I had plans for other tours, and had one scheduled with a professor from the seminary where Bro. Brown attended serving as a lecturer, which would have been a college credit course at MO Baptist College. However, the Yom Kippur war broke out and they cancelled all tours to Israel. The tour company was just another part of *the faulty foundation*.

God continued dealing with me. I tried to appease Him every way I could, but He continued speaking to my heart.

In **August of 1973**, I finally got to the point in my life where I was either going to have to surrender my life to the Lord, or just quit all the things I was trying to do to please him. I was at the point of back-sliding. I had never talked with my pastor, **Bro. A. B. Brown**, about my rebellion, so I went and talked with him about God's call on my life. He gave me some very wise advice, and that was to make sure, beyond a shadow of a doubt, that God was calling me into the ministry. He did not discourage me, but wanted me to make sure that I could do nothing but preach the Gospel. He had seen others, and I have too, who thought God was calling them to preach, but was mistaken about their calling.

On August 18, 1973, I went back and talked with Bro. Brown, after telling Ada of my talk with him concerning my calling, which she had not known about until then, and **I then surrendered to the Lordship of Christ in my life**. It was then that I quit building on *faulty foundations* with all my good works, and *laid a foundation stone for my life*. *1 Cor 3:11, For other foundation can no man lay than that is laid, which is Jesus Christ.*

I preached my first message on September 23, 1973, based on what I have shared with you thus far in this message. I enrolled in MO Baptist College in St. Louis, and went there my freshman year before completing college at Free Will Baptist College [now

Welch College] in Nashville.

I was re-baptized November 25, 1973, for I knew that previously, when dad baptized me, I was not totally right with the Lord. This concerned me, so I called my dad and told him I felt like I needed to be baptized, and he informed me that he was also re-baptized when he surrendered his life to the Lord when he was in his early 30's. Mom and Dad were happy that I had surrendered, as mom had been praying for a *'preacher boy'* from our family. Baptism is not only to signify what has happened in one's life, but what they are going to do after baptism—*walking in newness of life. (Rom 6:4-6, 13)*. Another *foundation stone* had been laid in my life.

June, 1974, we moved to Nashville, TN with our family to attend Bible College, leaving a good job at Dow Chemical, where I had worked for 17½ years. Many thought I was crazy to do what I was doing, but I knew I needed more Bible knowledge and didn't go to college to just get a degree like some obviously do. I started working as a DJ at WWGM, a religious radio station, the Monday after we moved to Nashville, but left there after two years because they started playing *'Jesus rock'* music, as I couldn't with a clear conscience play the music that sounded like worldly music. The pollution control business was now being run by Warren Livingston and helped to supplement my income while I attended Bible College.

May, 1977, I graduated from Free Will Baptist College [Welch College] with a B.A. degree and moved to Portsmouth, VA to serve as associate pastor at

Collinswood Free Will Baptist Church with **Bro. Jack Stallings**, with whom I served as a deacon when he pastored the church in Festus. While I was there I also had the opportunity to teach part-time at the Gateway Bible College, Virginia Beach, VA, and the college where Southeastern Free Will Bible College had its beginning. This was another answer to a question in my life concerning what God wanted me to do, as I had thought about going on to school so I could teach in college. I really enjoyed teaching, which is a lot less stressful than pastoring, but I knew this was not the will of God in my life. When we moved to Portsmouth, VA, Bro. Warren Livingston and I invested in a Christian bookstore, which prepared Bro. Warren for the position he later held as manager of the Lebanon Bible and Bookstore in Missouri.

In the fall of 1978 the Lord started dealing with me about trying to get a church to pastor. I talked with Bro. Stallings concerning this; he wanted me to stay and serve with him, but he said if I felt that was the Lord's will for my life, he would help me all he could. I tried out at several churches—I was to go to a church in Ohio and preach, but there was an ice storm and all the bridges and tunnels were closed getting out of Portsmouth—the sovereignty of God was again working for my good as I found out it was a troubled church. One church I tried out at in North Carolina lead me to believe they would be voting on the following Wednesday evening, and come to find out they had several who had come and preached and they had not voted on any of them.

I preached at a church in Cordova, AL, where a boy I

was in college with served as associate pastor. We had real good services that weekend and as I met with the board they all agreed with the standards and principles I stated concerning both their and my expectations. I was sure this was where the Lord wanted me to serve. When they called and said the vote was only 73% in favor of us coming, it surprised both me and their board, as they thought I would get well over 90% when I was with there with them before they voted on Wednesday evening.

I had went to the Bible Conference in Nashville the week before I had went to Cordova, AL, and **Dr. Joe Ange** told me about the church in Jackson, TN and encouraged me to stop by and look at the property on my way to visit our parents in Missouri. Also while I was at the conference Bro. Steve Pryor, pastoring in Selma, AL spoke to me about coming as a home missionary to Alabaster, AL. He didn't know that the Alabama Home Missions Board was also considering starting a mission work there and Bro. Bonnie Hughes, who served on the mission's board had also talked with me considering the new mission work. On the way to Missouri they had called me at my parent's home and wanted me to come and preach at Cordova.

After I was so sure we would be pastoring in Cordova, and I didn't get the vote I expected, as related earlier, I thought perhaps I was misreading God's will for my life and He wanted me to stay where I was at. Then on **Friday morning, April 6, 1979**, I prayed to the Lord to clearly reveal His will for my life. To open doors, or close doors, if He wanted me to stay in Portsmouth, VA. I was willing to stay, or if He wanted me to serve in missions, I was willing to do so. The secretary at the church happened to ask me that morning what I was planning to do. I told her I had prayed that morning and was leaving it in the hands of the Lord. I did not know that the Tennessee Home Missions Board happened to be meeting that same day, neither did I know they were considering me as a home missionary to come to Jackson, TN. Close to noon the telephone rang and it was Bro. Marion Pettus, the chairman of the Tennessee Home Missions Board, and he said they wanted me to come as a joint-project missionary to Jackson, TN. I told him I would need to come and preach and meet with the people before I could give them an answer. The church secretary happened to be in my office when the phone call came and said obviously the Lord had answered my prayer earlier that morning.

On Easter Sunday, April 15, 1979, we went to Jackson, TN, and all the family felt this was where the Lord wanted us to serve Him. There were 15 there that Sunday, counting our family and a boy from Nashville who had a crush on Sheila, and even less were back for the service that night, as one of the men who attended the church went fishing that evening. I met with the State Mission Board and the National Home Missions Board and they hired me as a joint-project missionary. Some thought I was not using very good judgment to leave the associate pastor position that was paying $21,400 a year, including the fringe benefits, to go to as a missionary, which was only $225 a week in pay. But we knew this was where we were to serve the Lord

We moved to Jackson, TN in June, 1979, and I started my missions itinerate the last weekend in June and had raised all the needed support by the first Sunday in October, even though the churches in Tennessee were already supporting two full time mission works in Tennessee. The week after we moved to Jackson a foreclosure on the property came in the mail. The Lord did some miraculous things financially while we were there and I had the privilege of being in the mortgage burning service when the church was totally debt-free. While I was on itinerate raising my support and away from the church on Sundays a young college student by the name of **James Forlines** came and very effectively filled the pulpit.

We remained at Jackson, TN for 10 years, and our family was down to just me and Ada, as Sheila and Matthew were married while we were there. We had a good ministry and some good people helping us. There were two good deacons that were a real support to me when I served the Lord in Jackson: **Bro. Laron Dye** and **Bro. Dan Morris**.

Bro. Dallas and Sis. Jerri Henderson moved to Jackson to help in the mission work. Dallas headed up our evangelism outreach, reaching many for the Lord. Some two years, previous to our leaving Jackson, TN before I felt the Lord was through with us there, I was contacted about turning my name in at the Farmington Free Will Baptist Church, as Bro. Jim McAllister was leaving to go to California Christian College, as their President. After consideration and prayer I didn't feel this was God's will and we needed to stay in Jackson, so I didn't send my name in to them.

When I did feel the Lord was through with us there in Jackson, TN, I told the church board, and did go and preach at several churches who were seeking a pastor— one in Oklahoma, two in Arkansas, one in Mississippi, two in Alabama, and one in Maryland. There were several who contacted me about coming that I prayed about and didn't go to try out—two in Florida, one in Hawaii, one in Illinois, one in Texas, one in Kansas, and one other church in Missouri, at Springfield, besides the church in Leadington, where we eventually moved to and started pastoring.

I went to Leadington Free Will Baptist Church for a week of revival, May 1-5, 1989, and the church elected me as their pastor, and started pastoring there the first Sunday in June. The first year at Leadington was really a trying of my faith, as in a little over a year there were 43 members who left the church and went somewhere else because of some problems that had developed in the church, that were already there when I started pastoring. After that first year and their leaving, the Lord started blessing our ministry at Leadington. We baptized 56 while pastoring there, which is nothing to brag about, as that only averaged seven a year in the eight years we were there. We did have an active '*Fishers of Men*' evangelism program and led many to the Lord.

In July of 1997, I knew the Lord was through with me at the Leadington Church. It surprised some on the church board, as well as Ada, when I turned my resignation in. I didn't have any church in mind when I resigned, but I knew God would open doors in accordance with His will. I went by and talked with **Bro. Roger Hogan** and told him I had resigned, and he wanted to know where I was going to pastor. I told him there was a church in Arkansas, and one in Ohio, that were looking for a pastor and that I was going to send a resume to them. Bro. Hogan said he hoped I would not leave Missouri and said while he pastored in Cape Girardeau that he felt we needed a church in Jackson, MO. He suggested I contact the MO State Missions Board concerning starting a mission work there. I contacted them and they met with me and came and looked over the area and hired me to come as a missionary, and we didn't miss one paycheck in the process. So we came and started looking for a place to live and a place to worship. The Lord worked in both situations, but we found a place to live before we found a place to worship. We were considering the old Church of Christ building on Old Cape Road and the party who was trying to buy it was having problems getting a loan, and we waited several weeks before we found out they were buying the building. I then started looking for a place to rent to worship in and found out what few places were available were too expensive to rent. By chance, or should I say, by God's will, I drove up Blanche Street and saw an old church building with a sign, Calvary Baptist Church. I found out who owned the building and called for a week and a half and just got a recording, as they were on vacation. When he did return my calls I asked him about the building and he said he was using it as a storage area for his business and was not planning to sell it. I called him back again and said I would like for the mission board to come and look at the building and make him an offer, which he agreed to. After they came and looked at the building and did some negotiating, they agreed to buy the building for $32,500. It was then that the tedious and long process of restoring the building began. We had help from many churches, as they came and worked on the building. We also received song books, the pulpit, all the way from Indiana, a communion set, and other things we needed to start a church. Then we had to find some pews, or some chairs to use. Again the Lord worked this out, and the mission board got the pews from Calvary Fellowship Free Will Baptist Church in Fenton, who were remodeling and buying new pews.

Bro. Dallas and Sis. Jerri Henderson moved to Jackson to help in the mission work [not a typographical error of what I said before] as they again moved to help in the mission work in Jackson, MO. We had an active *'Evangelism Explosion'* program and led several to the Lord. Another couple who came and helped us was **John and Gail Rhodes** with their son Randall. They were involved in the youth program and evangelism.

I have shared all this, and could share a lot more about those who helped with the building, as well as the first seven who were in our first informal service, and those who came to those first services to follow, to show how the will of God was confirmed in my life. I have highlighted some of the major events in my life and those who had an influence on my life.

Earlier in my life I was laying *faulty foundations,* which would not endure the storms of life, but now I know Who my foundation is on, and I better take heed as to how I build thereon. Some verses I use in a message, *'A Secure Foundation'* says, **For we are labourers together with God: ye are God's husbandry, ye are God's building. According to the grace of God which is given unto me, as a wise masterbuilder, I have laid the foundation, and another buildeth thereon. But let every man take heed how he buildeth thereupon. For other foundation can no man lay than that is laid, which is Jesus Christ, 1 Cor 3:9-11**

After 11½ of pastoring the **Jackson Free Will Baptist Church** I felt it was time to retire. Ada was looking forward to our retirement. When Ada passed away she received *'a retirement plan out of this world.'* After my retirement was when we started attending the **First Free Will Baptist Church in Cape Girardeau**. They did accept us generously. I appreciate all the intercessory prayers that they and others have prayed for me since the **passing of Ada, April 18, 2015**. She was *'one of a kind'*, but the kind I needed for 59 years. Be sure to read my tribute to her concerning her faithfulness as a wife; as a mother; and as a pastor's wife.

Application of message: The point of giving my personal testimony is not to boast of anything I have done, as a matter of fact, I sure have nothing to boast about with all my earlier rebellion against the Lord. The point is this, every one of you know whether you are in God's will for your life, and if you are not, I don't care what you may be doing, it is a *faulty foundation* that you are building your life on, if you are not building it on the foundation of Christ, and His Lordship in your life.

In the days we are living in we must have *'a secure foundation'*. How do you face the rains, the floods and the ill winds which blow your way in this life? Maybe you need to reestablish yourself on the Rock Jesus Christ. Maybe you have never came to the **Lord** before and your life has been established on the shifting sands of this world—you need to come and start building your life on the solid foundation of Jesus. Maybe your life is a mess and it is about ready to crumble and fall like the foolish man's house did. If you were to die today, what would be the result of your final test? Let me tell you the *'Good News,'* what the Gospel, believed and received in your heart will do for you. It will make a new house for you to live in--*2 Cor 5:17, Therefore if any man be in Christ, he is a new creature* [creation]: *old things are passed away; behold, all things are become new*. Why would anyone turn away from such an offer?

Listen again to *Mat 7:24-27, Therefore whosoever heareth these sayings of mine, and doeth them, I will liken him unto a wise man, which built his house upon a rock: and the rain descended, and the floods came, and the winds blew, and beat upon that house; and it fell not: for it was founded upon a rock. And every one that heareth these sayings of mine, and doeth them not, shall be likened unto a foolish man, which built his house upon the sand: and the rain descended, and the floods came, and the winds blew, and beat upon that house; and it fell: and great was the fall of it.*.

What FWB Believe About Giving Ourselves

I Thess.1:1-6

¹ *Paul, and Silvanus, and Timotheus, unto the church of the Thessalonians which is in God the Father and in the Lord Jesus Christ: Grace be unto you, and peace, from God our Father, and the Lord Jesus Christ.*
² *We give thanks to God always for you all, making mention of you in our prayers;*
³ *Remembering without ceasing your work of faith, and labour of love, and patience of hope in our Lord Jesus Christ, in the sight of God and our Father;*
⁴ *Knowing, brethren beloved, your election of God.*
⁵ *For our gospel came not unto you in word only, but also in power, and in the Holy Ghost, and in much assurance; as ye know what manner of men we were among you for your sake.*
⁶ *And ye became followers of us, and of the Lord, having received the word in much affliction, with joy of the Holy Ghost:*

On the back of your bulletin is our Church Covenant, and it will be the emphasis in the messages in the coming weeks. In a revival I preached I was led of the Lord to preach on the Covenant. I have revival messages that I could have preached and I told the pastor how the Lord was leading me, and he said I better be obedient to the Lord and it was what the church needed.

I appreciate the favorable comments of those who have asked to receive these messages on the internet. A veteran missionary wrote, *I appreciate the emphasis you are giving to doctrine. We need more of that and less feel good, buttery, psychology in our churches today.* A veteran pastor wrote,

I want to commend you for teaching your congregation what Free Will Baptist believe. Too few pastors perform this needed instruction.

A covenant is an agreement entered into by two or more parties in which they consent to mutually carry out together certain provisions contained in the document. A more common covenant is the marriage covenant, when two people are joined in Holy Matrimony and exchange their wedding vows. This is one of the more broken covenants of our day, as over 50% of marriages do not last *'until death do us part.'* A covenant then is *'giving ourselves'* to one another, or others. We will see the giving ourselves clearly in the Preamble of our covenant, which is the part of the covenant I will preach from today [read]. A church covenant is not peculiar to FWB, as other church groups have covenants quite similar to ours. Our covenant was adopted at the General Conference of FWB in 1832 and has remained unchanged since that time. There are some in our ranks who have favored changing the covenant, but I believe as a covenant it sets forth what our Treatise of Faith and Practices says that we *do b*elieve. Covenants between God and man date back to Genesis and one of the more familiar covenants which we are reminded of every time we see a rainbow, is God's covenant after the flood. The rainbow is a *'token'* [sign] of God's covenant. The word *'covenant' i*s used 292 times in the Bible. Our Treatise states that those who wish to become members of a FWB church are to adopt our covenant. This is the reason why I will always read it when anyone presents themselves as candidates for church membership. There are many areas of the Christian life covered by the covenant; some areas which are too often being neglected in our day. They are even being neglected in many of our pulpits as some pastors are not preaching God's Word like FWB have preached in the past. Consequently, we have many in our churches who do not know such a covenant exists, and if they do know it, they are not living it because its principles are not being preached from the pulpit. The taking of a covenant should *solemnize t*he entrance into such a covenant, whether it is at the marriage altar, or when a believer becomes a member of a local church. The FWB Church Covenant does not set forth doctrine, but it does set forth some principles which should be adopted by every believer in Christ. So this message is for everyone here, whether you are a FWB, one who has not yet joined a church, or an unsaved person--to show you the true meaning of repentance. I have entitled the message, *'What FWB Believe About Giving Ourselves,'* as the Preamble of our covenant clearly states a giving of ourselves to God and a giving of ourselves to one another [read again]. My text is *1 Thess.1:1-6.* There are three things I want you to see in the first section of our Covenant in giving yourselves to God and to one another:

I. First and foremost, there must be a giving of ourselves to God. *(Rom. 12:1,2)* There must be the saving faith which enables us to give ourselves to Him. Giving ourselves to God means taking Christ as Savior and Lord. Note we do this by *'faith in Jesus Christ.'* I do not take much stock in a person who says they have been saved and yet have not given themselves to God. The Lord must always be first in our lives, if we are really living for Him. Faith is trust. When we put our faith in Christ we are forgiven and born again. This is the only way we can give ourselves to God. *'Having given ourselves to God, by faith in Christ'.* That opening statement is a testimony of our salvation through the Lord Jesus Christ and a declaration to all that we have repented of our sins, accepted Christ by faith as Savior, and have become new creatures in Christ Jesus. We are **'hid with Christ in God,' (Col 3:3)** and are no longer our own, for we are **'bought with a price,' 1 Cor 6:20.** We thus testify to the existence of an eternal God, the virgin-born Son of God, whose blood cleanses us from all sin, and the Holy Spirit, Who convicted us of sin and pointed us to Christ, and continues to guide us.

Paul commended the Macedonians—*2 Cor.8:5, they, first gave themselves to the Lord, and unto us by the will of God.* That will keep you from getting *'preacher religion,'* for if you first give yourselves to God, you will then work in the will of the Lord, and not just because the preacher says to do it. It will also help you to not be deceived by those who come *'in word only'* *(v.5)* I not only believe in a saving faith in giving ourselves to God, but I also believe in a keeping faith, which appropriates the grace of God and is expressed in a changed life, as we daily give ourselves to God. The only way you can experience His grace is by continually *'giving yourself to God.'*

II. Secondly, we find the importance of Scripture, after we have given ourselves to God. *(2 Tim.2:15)* Application of the Word of God in your daily living. Giving ourselves to God automatically means *'adopting the Word of God as our rule of faith and practice.'* You cannot claim to choose God without choosing what He has said in His Word. The Bible contains the only way and the whole description of our duties toward God and one another. What does Paul tell the Thessalonian believers *(v.6)?* It was after their receiving the Word that they became followers of the missionaries and the Lord they served. *Faith cometh by hearing, and hearing by the Word of God, Rom.10: 17.* If you have never received this Word as the very Word of God, as though He is speaking to you audibly, then you have never *'adopted the Word of God as your rule of faith and practice.'* You must acknowledge the Bible to be the [God-breathed] inspired Word of God, *written by holy men as they were moved by the Holy Ghost (2 Pet.1:21).* When you promise in the covenant to adopt the Word of God, it means you accept the Bible as your rule in life, vowing that you will live according to its instructions, walk in its precepts, obey its commandments, trust in its promises, and teach it to others. To adopt it as your rule of faith and practice means you will uphold it by all means, defend it against the ungodly, and will declare its counsels by daily lives of devotion and godliness. You are an *'epistle known and read of all men' (2 Cor.3:2) a*nd how sad it is when they read *'Christians' w*hose lives do not match up with the rule of faith and practice as declared in God's Word. Far too many in our day have not *'adopted the Word of God as their rule of faith and practice.'* Too many are getting their faith and practice from another gospel, which is not the true Gospel. The Word of God is sacred and is the revelation of God to man concerning what he needs to know about God, how to be saved, how to live for the Lord and how to go to heaven when he dies, rather than a devil's hell. That makes this Book an important Book and we had better be careful how we treat it in respect to how we live, if we claim to be Christians. Nothing is to supersede the Word of God as an authority for faith and practice. No church doctrine or creed supersedes this Book. If FWB should go liberal and change its doctrines and beliefs, it will be because they try to change what this Book says. We had better be careful to not try to change this eternal, infallible, inspired, inerrant, eternal Word of God. Man cannot change the Word of God, no matter how educated he may become, or how many per-versions he writes. Instead of trying to change the Bible, men need to allow the Bible to change them. In this first message on our Church Covenant, I ask you, have you *'adopted the Word of God as your rule of faith and practice?'*

III. Thirdly, we are to give ourselves to one another by the will of God. This is real Christian living, as we do not live for ourselves but we live for others. *Giving ourselves to one another is* the whole covenant in a nutshell. If we could just perfectly live up to this, the church would be paradise on earth. But while the church certainly isn't perfect, every believer ought to aim at giving himself unreservedly to his fellow believers. Giving yourself to others means not only giving of yourself to those who are always living in God's will, but also to those who may fall into sin *(Gal. 6:1,2; Rom.14:1; 15:1)* The Bible lays a solid foundation for the commitment of giving ourselves one to another. *'By one Spirit are all baptized into one body,' I Cor.12:13.* The *'body' is* often used, comparing the church to the human body. The church is also called a 'household' *(Gal.6:10; Eph.2:19),* which means a family. Sometimes the church is called a *'building,' a 'living temple' w*here God dwells *(1 Cor.3:9-17; Eph.2:19-22).*

The oneness that comes about by giving ourselves to one another is also seen in the ways the Bible expresses our relationship to each other. One of the most impressive of these is stated in *Eph.4:25, Wherefore putting away lying, speak every man truth with his neighbour: for we are members one of another.* It says in *Rom 12:5. So we, being many, are one body in Christ, and every one members one of another. Gi*ving ourselves to one another, then, means we see our need of each other and say we will serve each other.

That is the *'brotherly love'* spoken of in Scripture. Brotherly love is promoting a brother's [sister's] welfare, even at one's own expense *(Phil.2:3,4).* When we give ourselves to one another it does involve more that fun and fellowship [and I like fun and fellowship]. Listen to *1 Thess.1:3.* This is what giving ourselves to one another is about. Do you know what the word *'work'* means there in Greek? *'To work, put forth an effort, to be doing, to act.'* This is that keeping faith I mentioned earlier. We are not saved by works, nor are we kept by works, but if we are saved, we will work *(Eph.2:10 follows vv.8,9) James 2:17, Even so faith, if it hath not works, is dead, being alone.* So giving ourselves to one another involves work and when there is work to be done, help others do what needs to be done. What do you think *'labor'* means in the Greek language? Another startling revelation--it means labor. It means doing something that is painful, when it brings weariness, when you are already tired, when it may be inconvenient. That is a labor of love, when you don't feel like doing it, you do it anyway. *(Heb.6:8-12).*

What does *'patience'* mean in the original language? It means just that, endurance, hopeful, constancy. It means *'hanging in there.'* It means not getting discouraged when it seems nothing is being accomplished. It means doing it whether anyone else does it or not. It involves soul winning *(Luke 8:15).* I want you to note the last two words of this first paragraph of our church covenant—*'this solemn covenant.'* Solemn means, serious, grave, deeply earnest. It is not to be taken lightly! It is by the *'will of*

*God' t*hat we bind ourselves together. We give ourselves to one another because we have given ourselves to God, because we have *'adopted the Word of God as our rule of faith and practice.'*

Having said all this about the Preamble of our Church Covenant, I come back to what I said in the beginning, this message is for everyone here. There must first be salvation, then comes the Lordship of Christ, as we do what He tells us to do in His Word. Have you ever given yourself to God, by faith in Jesus Christ? Have you accepted Christ, but you are not living according to this Book? It has not been the rule of faith and practice in your life? Have you given yourself to others in the church? Have you given the Gospel to lost people, not only in word, but in practice, being a living epistle of the Word of God? Have you given yourself to others by praying for and witnessing to the lost you know? Will you make a covenant with the Lord?

This is one of the 5 messages on the Church Covenant from the 'What Do Free Will Baptists Believe' series available on the 'Monitor Messages' CD.

The Intermediate State of Death
1 Cor.15:35-38; 42-44

[35] But some *man* will say, How are the dead raised up? and with what body do they come?

[36] T*hou* fool, that which thou sowest is not quickened, except it die:

[37] And that which thou sowest, thou sowest not that body that shall be, but bare grain, it may chance of wheat, or of some other *grain*:

[38] But God giveth it a body as it hath pleased him, and to every seed his own body.

[42] So also *is* the resurrection of the dead. It is sown in corruption; it is raised in incorruption:

[43] It is sown in dishonour; it is raised in glory: it is sown in weakness; it is raised in power:

[44] It is sown a natural body; it is raised a spiritual body. There is a natural body, and there is a spiritual body.

In the last message I preached from *vv. 54-57* concerning the sting of death. I said in the message that we are all going to die, unless the Lord comes back to rapture us. Death is a subject that man doesn't like to think about, and you may be saying, *'Preacher, get off the subject of death and preach about more pleasant things'.* If you are a believer you don't have to worry and fret about dying, because Christ took the stinger of the scorpion of death at Calvary and a scorpion may be a horrible looking creature but without a stinger it is harmless. Now if you are unsaved, or you have unforgiven sin in your life you have a right to fear death and the horrible creatures of *Rev. 9* who will sting and torture people for 5 months. Men will try to kill themselves because of the pain of the sting. They **shall desire to die, and death shall flee from them.(6).** The subject I am preaching on today is not preached about much because the Bible doesn't tell us a whole lot about it. We hear messages on death and on the 2nd Coming and the rapture, which I will cover in the messages to follow, but how many messages have you heard concerning the intermediate state of death from the time you die until you receive your new resurrection body at the rapture.

The *conscious state of happiness or misery* is what this message is about.

The place and condition of the dead between death and the resurrection is called the intermediate state. It deals with the question, where does one go immediately when he dies? I've already established why we must die in *Rom 5:12, Wherefore, as by one man sin entered into the world, and death by sin; and so death passed upon all men, for that all have sinned.* The text in the previous message said, *1 Cor 15:56, The sting of death is sin; and the strength of sin is the law. The sting of death is sin* because sin is death's cause and punishment. As believers we can say, *O death, where is thy sting? O grave, where is thy victory? 1 Cor 15:55.* And why can we say that? *v.57, But thanks be to God, which giveth us the victory through our Lord Jesus Christ.* Having said that we must die *Rom 6:23, For the wages of sin is death,* I want to give the hope we have because *the gift of God is eternal life through Jesus Christ our Lord.*

The last sentence of this section of our Treatise: *The soul does not die with the body, but immediately after death enters into a conscious state of happiness or misery, according to the character here possessed.* This is what I want to base my message on. Earlier we sang, *'Where the Soul of Man Never Dies'.* I hope you will see the truth of that song, as well as the truth that you will be in a conscious state for eternity and it is in your life time here on earth, by your character, you chose whether it will be a state of happiness or misery!

I. The soul of man does not die. The cults teach that you are just like other animal life, when you are dead, you are dead, but what does the Bible say?

Eccl 3:19-21, For that which befalleth the sons of men befalleth beasts; even one thing befalleth them: as the one dieth, so dieth the other; yea, they have all one breath; so that a man hath no preeminence above a beast: for all is vanity. All go unto one place; all are of the dust, and all turn to dust again. The cults stop reading here, but note *v.21, Who knoweth the spirit of man that goeth upward, and the spirit of the beast that goeth downward to the earth? 12:7, Then shall the dust return to the earth as it was: and the spirit shall return unto God who gave it.*

It is always amazing to me how the Lord supplies helps for my messages as I study and prepare. Friday's devotion in Days of Praise was from *1 Cor 15:42, So also is the resurrection of the dead. It is sown in corruption; it is raised in incorruption.* It said, and I quote: *When a believer's soul and spirit leave the body and return to the Lord, it is significant that New Testament Scriptures speak of the body, not as dead, but as sleeping. For example, Jesus said, 'Our friend Lazarus sleepeth; but I go, that I may awake him out of sleep' John 11:11. This state is not 'soul sleep' as some teach, for 'to be absent from the body, [is] to be present with the Lord' (2 Cor 5:8). The body is sleeping--not the soul. Similarly, when the believer's body is laid in a grave, Paul speaks of this act not as a burial, but as sowing! 1 Cor. 15:35-38, 'But some man will say, How are the dead raised up? And with what body do they come? Thou fool, that which thou sowest is not quickened, except it die: and that which thou sowest, thou sowest not that body that shall be, but bare grain, it may chance of wheat, or of some other grain: But God giveth it a body as it hath pleased Him, and to every seed his own body'. Just as a buried grain of wheat brings forth a fruitful plant, so the old, sin-corrupted, aching body of human flesh, sown in the ground, will someday come forth 'fashioned like unto His glorious body' Phil 3:21, in which 'there shall be no more death, neither sorrow, nor crying, neither shall there be any more pain',Rev 21:4.*

1 Cor 15:42-44 'So also is the resurrection of the dead. It is sown in corruption; it is raised in incorruption: It is sown in dishonor; it is raised in glory: it is sown in weakness; it is raised in power: It is sown a natural body; it is raised a spiritual body'. When a believer's body is sown in the ground, God will soon reap from it a body of glory which will last for eternity-- Henry Morris.

Men fail to distinguish the difference between the resurrection of the body and the immortality of the soul. The Sadducees denied any resurrection, any life after death. But Christ countered their argument that **God is not the God of the dead, but of the living. (Matt. 22:32).** One commentary says the name of the Sadducees describes their condition, as they were *'sad you see'* in not believing in the resurrection.

I answered in the previous message, What is death? Death is a separation. It is not the ending of the spirit or of the personality. These do not die. The real *'you'* goes on to be with the Lord if you are a child of God. It is the body that disintegrates. Death is a separation of the body from the individual, from the person. The body disintegrates, decays, decomposes. Dust to dust and ashes to ashes applies only to the body. As we have read, when the body is buried it is compared to seed planted. I did a search on *'seed germination'* on the internet and found there to be 1,930,000 sites on the subject, so rather than look at all of them I choose what the first one said: *A seed certainly looks dead. It does not seem to move, to grow, nor do anything. In fact, even with biochemical tests for the metabolic processes we associate with life (respiration, etc.) the rate of these processes is so slow that it would be difficult to determine whether there really was anything alive in a seed. Indeed if a seed is not allowed to germinate (sprout) within some certain length of time, the embryo inside will die.* So Paul says that our bodies are like that seed that is planted, it is dead. ***1 Cor 15:42-44, It is sown in corruption; it is raised in incorruption: it is sown in dishonour; it is raised in glory: it is sown in weakness; it is raised in power: it is sown a natural body; it is raised a spiritual body. There is a natural body, and there is a spiritual body.*** Though our natural bodies will be dead, there is that eternal part of man that lives for eternity.

Today is 'Sanctity of Life' Sunday and it is the 33rd anniversary of the infamous decision by the Supreme Court on January 22, 1973 to legalize abortion—the murder of the unborn.

The Bible is very clear that life begins at conception and all those innocent babies I believe are presently with Jesus. They may not have been given a proper burial and placed as a seed in the ground, none the less they are planted and will one day receive a body that is ***fashioned like unto Christ's glorious body, Phil 3:21.*** I will be saying more on the abortion issue in this evening's message, *'The State of the Union in 2003'.*

II. There are two truths revealed in the Scriptures about the state of the dead that need to be emphasized to those who are now living. As I said earlier, there is not much Scripture that deals with the intermediate state of death—from the time we die until the time of receiving our new bodies. The Treatise states it well—*immediately after death one enters into a conscious state of happiness or misery.* The Bible doesn't say much, but it says enough for us to know there is a consciousness after death.

A. First, it is clear that the righteous are in a state of conscious existence with the Lord. Paul wrote that when we die we will be with Jesus in *Phil 1:23, For I am in a strait betwixt two, having a desire to depart, and to be with Christ; which is far better* and in *2 Cor 5:8, We are confident, I say, and willing rather to be absent from the body, and to be present with the Lord.* That there is a state of conscious existence is strongly implied in Jesus telling about the rich man and Lazarus. He says of Lazarus, *And it came to pass, that the beggar died, and was carried by the angels into Abraham's bosom Luke 16:22* and it also says in *v. 25, now he is comforted.* Paul's *'to depart, and to be with Christ'* can hardly be explained if he did not think that he would have a conscious existence after he departed. As Jesus was on the cross paying the death penalty for our sins, He said to the repentant thief hanging beside Him, *Verily I say unto thee, To day shalt thou be with me in paradise, Luke 23:43.* Jesus the Son of God, would not lie to this dying thief, nor to us, about our being with Him at our death.

Paul writes that we are going to be with Him as we come on the resurrection morning to receive our new bodies *1 Th 4:14, For if we believe that Jesus died and rose again, even so them also which sleep in Jesus will God bring with him.* When it says that we *sleep in Jesus* that in no way teaches soul sleep, where there is no consciousness. The word *'sleep'* there means that as believers we are *'dead in Christ.'*

B. Second, it is clear that the unrighteous will have a state of conscious existence apart from God immediately after death. This is clearly taught in Jesus telling about the rich man and Lazarus. Let's read it in *Lk 16:19 -31.* We find here repeated references to feelings and consciousness. He saw *(v. 23) And in hell he lift up his eyes, being in torments, and seeth Abraham afar off, and Lazarus in his bosom;* he spake *v. 24 And he cried and said, Father Abraham, have mercy on me, and send Lazarus, that he may dip the tip of his finger in water, and cool my tongue; for I am tormented in this flame;* he felt *v. 23, being in torments; I am tormented in this flame,v.24;* he remembered *v. 25 But Abraham said, Son, remember that thou in thy lifetime receivedst thy good things, and likewise Lazarus evil things: but now he is comforted, and thou art tormented;* and he was conscious of what was going on in earth *v. 27-28, Then he said, I pray thee therefore, father, that thou wouldest send him to my father's house: for I have five brethren; that he may testify unto them, lest they also come into this place of torment.* The conscious fires of hell will be miserable, but the misery of hell will be the fact of all these senses will still be present with unbelievers.

III. Man now has a choice in the matter of where he will go when he dies. *The soul does not die with the body, but immediately after death enters into a conscious state of happiness or misery, according to the character here possessed.* Whether you will be in a state of happiness or misery will depend upon your character when you die. It tells us in *Eccl 11:3. . if the tree fall toward the south, or toward the north, in the place where the tree falleth, there it shall be.* So it is when we die! Our eternal state is settled once for all.

Both the saved and unsaved will experience a resurrection, as Jesus states in *John 5:28, 29, Marvel not at this: for the hour is coming, in the which all that are in the graves shall hear his voice, and shall come forth; they that have done good, unto the resurrection of life; and they that have done evil, unto the resurrection of damnation.* The resurrection of life for believers will happen at the rapture of the church as related in *1 Th 4:13-18.* If you are living when the rapture occurs and have not received *'the love of the truth, that you might be saved'* then the Bible says your eternal fate has been sealed and you will suffer physically the wrath of God during the great tribulation. *2 Th. 2:8-12, And then shall that Wicked be revealed, whom the Lord shall consume with the spirit of his mouth, and shall destroy with the brightness of his coming: even him, whose coming is after the working of Satan with all power and signs and lying wonders, and with all deceivableness of unrighteousness in them that perish; because they received not the love of the truth, that they might be saved. And for this cause God shall send them strong delusion, that they should believe a lie: that they all might be damned who believed not the truth, but had pleasure in unrighteousness.* If you die lost you will immediately go to hell and you will continue be there when the saved will reign with Christ here on earth for a thousand years. *But the rest of the dead lived not again until the thousand years were finished. This is the first resurrection. Blessed and holy is he that hath part in the first resurrection: on such the second death hath no power, Rev 20:5,6.* The *resurrection of damnation* of those suffering in hell will happen after the Millennial Reign of Christ at the Great White Throne Judgment as related in *Rev 20:10-15, And the devil that deceived them was cast into the lake of fire and brimstone, where the beast and the false prophet are, and shall be tormented day and night for ever and ever. And I saw a great white throne, and him that sat on it, from whose face the earth and the heaven fled away; and there was found no place for them. And I saw the dead, small and great, stand before God; and the books were opened: and another book was opened, which is the book of life: and the dead were judged out of those things which were written in the books, according to their works. And the sea gave up the dead which were in it; and death and hell delivered up the dead which were in them: and they were judged every man according to their works. And death and hell were cast into the lake of fire. This is the second death. And whosoever was not found written in the book of life was cast into the lake of fire.*

Is your name in the Book of Life? You have a choice today! If you were to die today do you know for sure you would go to be in the presence of Jesus at the moment that life passes from your body? What will be your decision today? In closing, listen once again to what we as Free Will Baptists believe concerning death: *As a result of sin, all mankind is subject to the death of the body. The soul does not die with the body, but immediately after death enters into a conscious state of happiness or misery, according to the character here possessed.*

Footnote: This message has more meaning to me than it did when I first preached it in 2003. A few months ago my wife Ada went home to be with the Lord, April 18, 2015. Her physical life was one of pain with crippling arthritis for some 50 years. I know she is ***now comforted*** as Lazarus is from his ***body full of sores.*** Ada is awaiting the resurrection morning when she will receive her new body ***'that it may be fashioned like unto his glorious body', Phil 3:21.*** Ada is now present with the Lord in a *'conscience state of happiness'.* She is now rejoicing ***'in the presence of angels'*** every time souls are saved around the world, for it tells us in ***Luke 15:10, Likewise, I say unto you, there is joy in the presence of the angels of God over one sinner that repenteth.***

This is one of the 80 messages from the 'What Do Free Will Baptists Believe' series available on the CD, and also available on 'Monitor Messages' CD.

The Revelation of Jesus Christ
Rev 1:8, 11, 17b-20

[8] I am Alpha and Omega, the beginning and the ending, saith the Lord, which is, and which was, and which is to come, the Almighty.

[11] Saying, I am Alpha and Omega, the first and the last: and, What thou seest, write in a book, and send *it* unto the seven churches which are in Asia; unto Ephesus, and unto Smyrna, and unto Pergamos, and unto Thyatira, and unto Sardis, and unto Philadelphia, and unto Laodicea.

[17] And when I saw him, I fell at his feet as dead. And he laid his right hand upon me, saying unto me, Fear not; I am the first and the last:

[18] I *am* he that liveth, and was dead; and, behold, I am alive for evermore, Amen; and have the keys of hell and of death.

[19] Write the things which thou hast seen, and the things which are, and the things which shall be hereafter;

[20] The mystery of the seven stars which thou sawest in my right hand, and the seven golden candlesticks. The seven stars are the angels of the seven churches: and the seven candlesticks which thou sawest are the seven churches.

I have been studying on the church at Ephesus and up until Friday evening had planned to start preaching on the churches this evening. However, the Lord has directed otherwise and I will preach another introductory message of the 7 churches addressed in Revelation. In the introduction to the previous message I said that the theme of Revelation is Jesus Christ victorious! The title is *'The Revelation of Jesus Christ'*. It is not the *'Revelation of St. John the Divine'* as some Bible falsely title it, nor is it *'Revelations'* as some call it...it is one revelation and it is all about Jesus . Revelation-*'apokalupsis'* is the Greek word meaning, *'an uncovering, an unveiling or a disclosure'*. It is *'The Revelation of Jesus Christ'*. So I want to deal with His revelation to the 7 churches, which I believe will help you to better understand His revelation to the churches of our day. My text for this message are the sayings of Christ in **chap. 1** **o**f **vv.8, 11, 17b-20.** I said in an earlier message to those of you who have a red-letter Bible it is the words of Christ from **Rev.2:1** through **3:22.** So we see that these 7 epistles are directly from Jesus to the churches. I want to specifically point out how Christ reveals Himself to the 7 churches.

I. Jesus reveals Himself to the seven churches. He does not appear to all alike. He approaches each in some special character. That is what I want you to see in this message.

(1) **T**o Ephesus he appears as one unto the angel of the church as *'He that holdeth the seven stars in his right hand, who walketh in the midst of the seven golden candlesticks,' Rev 2:1.*

(2) To Smyrna he appears as *'the first and the last, which was dead, and is alive,' Rev 2:8.*

(3) To Pergamos he appears as *'He which hath the sharp sword with two edges,' Rev 2:12.*

(4) To Thyatira as *'the Son of God, who hath his eyes like unto a flame of fire, and his feet are like fine brass,' Rev 2:18.*

(5) To Sardis He appears as *'He that hath the seven Spirits of God, and the seven stars,' Rev 3:1.*

(6) To Philadelphia as *'He that is holy, he that is true, he that hath the key of David, he that openeth, and no man shutteth; and shutteth, and no man openeth, Rev 3:7*

(7) To Laodicea as *'the Amen, the faithful and true witness, the beginning of the creation of God,' Rev 3:14.*

The letters were addressed to the messengers of the church, but the epistles were written to the saints in the churches. In all of the epistles Jesus addresses Himself through a special person—**unto the angel of the church.** Who is **the angel of the church?** Most commentaries agree this was the appointed messenger of the little community — the pastor, the one who had received the letter from John, who had received it by inspiration from God. *All scripture is given by inspiration of God, and is profitable for doctrine, for reproof, for correction, for instruction in righteousness, 2 Tim 3:16.* I believe you will see in these epistles to the 7 churches that are inspired (God-breathed), the very words of Christ will be *profitable for doctrine, for reproof, for correction, for instruction in righteousness.*

II. The Lord Jesus Christ presented Himself differently in the salutations to the churches for a reason. The description is always significant in view of the condition of each of the seven churches. **(1)** *The church in Ephesus,* Christ was the one **that holdeth the seven stars in his right hand, who walketh in the midst of the seven golden candlesticks,' Rev 2:1.** The chief characteristic of this church was she had left her first love. **(2)** Christ presented Himself to the *church in Smyrna* as **'the first and the last, which was dead, and is alive,' Rev 2:8.** Her chief characteristic was suffering. **(3)** To the *church in Pergamum,* He was the one **which hath the sharp sword with two edges,' Rev 2:12.** This was a lax church, the seat of Satan's authority. **(4)** Christ made Himself known to the *church in Thyatira* as **'the Son of God, who hath his eyes like unto a flame of fire, and his feet are like fine brass,' Rev 2:18.** Thyatira's chief characteristic was tolerating Jezebel, a false teacher. **(5)** He revealed Himself to *the church in Sardis* as **'He that hath the seven Spirits of God, and the seven stars,' Rev 3:1.** Her chief characteristic was a reputation that she was alive, but she was in a dead state. **(6)** The Lord Jesus spoke to the *church in Philadelphia* as **'He that is holy, he that is true, he that hath the key of David, he that openeth, and no man shutteth; and shutteth, and no man openeth, Rev 3:7** She was loyal to Christ's word and refused to deny His name. **(7)** Christ revealed Himself to *the church in Laodicea* as **'the Amen, the faithful and true witness, the beginning of the creation of God,' Rev 3:14.** This church had the characteristics of lukewarm-ness and self-complacency.

III. What was *the revelation of Jesus Christ* in these statements to the churches?

A. in Ephesus Jesus Christ is holding the stars—angels or messengers—in His right hand. These messengers are called stars. *Rev 1:20 The mystery of the seven stars which thou sawest in my right hand, and the seven golden candle-sticks. The seven stars are the angels of the seven churches: and the seven candle-sticks which thou sawest are the seven churches.* The light reflected from the messenger does not originate with the messenger. As we look up in the sky at night we may say the stars are shining, but they are only reflecting the light of the sun. As messengers, or witnesses we are reflecting the light of the Son of God. The stars, or the messengers, are in the protecting and controlling hand of Him Who calls and ordains. The right hand denotes one who is on the offense. Christ is on the offense. When the high priest at the crucifixion of Christ questioned Jesus, *whether thou be the Christ, the Son of God. Jesus saith unto him, Thou hast said: nevertheless I say unto you, hereafter shall ye see the Son of man sitting on the right hand of power, and coming in the clouds of heaven. Mat 26:63,64.* At the right hand is a place of authority. *Acts 5:31 Him hath God exalted with his right hand to be a Prince and a Saviour, for to give repentance to Israel, and forgiveness of sins.*

The two words *'holdeth'* and *'walketh'*, are present active participles. The Lord is presently calling, ordaining, and holding the true messenger of each particular church in His hand. And Christ is walking in the midst of the lamp-stands. Walking must be distinguished from sitting. After finishing the work the Father sent Him to perform, Jesus Christ sat down at the Father's right hand. Sitting denotes intercession on behalf of His people and walking denotes judgment. The coming kingdom is in full view with Christ's present judgment of the churches. If one *'leaves their first love'* as Ephesus did they will be judged for it. This judgment is related to the removal of the lampstand or candlestick, which is the church. Many a denominational churches who have left their first love are no more, as far as God is concerned. Am I being judgmental when I say some have left their first love. No, for it tells us in *1 John 5:2,3 By this we know that we love the children of God, when we love God, and keep his commandments. For this is the love of God, that we keep his commandments: and his commandments are not grievous.*

B. Jesus Christ was presented to the church in Smyrna as the One who is the first and the last, who was dead and is alive forevermore. Her chief characteristic was suffering. His suffering comforted the suffering saints in Smyrna. Christ's assertion that He is the first and the last taught His eternal existence to those saints. Smyrna is the Greek form of the Hebrew word *myrrh that* sweet fragrant spice so largely used in connection with burials.

The sweet fragrance of these saints was pressed out by their affliction. Myrrh was one of the spices brought by the wise men to the baby Jesus Christ. They brought gold, frankincense, and myrrh. The gold spoke of His deity, frankincense of His impeccable humanity, and myrrh of His death. Myrrh was also used to prepare the body of our Lord for burial

His salutation disarmed the fears of the suffering saints in Smyrna. He assured them that He is the first and the last, the one who became dead and lives. He assured the suffering saints in Smyrna that they were in His hands and the Devil could not try them any more than their blessed Captain allowed. Every circumstance to which Christians are subjected is in the will of Jesus Christ, the Captain of their salvation. These suffering saints did not know what the future held for them, but they knew who held the future.

C. In the salutation to the church in Pergamum the Lord Jesus is described as the One who has the sharp two-edged sword. *Rev 1:16* ties together what is said of Smyrna and Pergamum--*And he had in his right hand seven stars: and out of his mouth went a sharp twoedged sword: and his countenance was as the sun shineth in his strength.* The One who has the sharp two-edged sword was an appropriate description in view of Christ's complaint against the church in Pergamum. This was a lax church, the seat of Satan's authority. Christ is described as the Word of God. It tells us of the Word of God in *Heb 4:12 For the word of God is quick, and powerful, and sharper than any twoedged sword, piercing even to the dividing asunder of soul and spirit, and of the joints and marrow, and is a discerner of the thoughts and intents of the heart.* The written or spoken word is called the sword of the Spirit: *"...the sword of the Spirit, which is the word of God" (Eph. 6:17)*. The sword of the Lord cuts two ways. It is capable of both direct and backstrokes. The former is for conviction, and the latter is for punishment.

D. The Lord presented Himself to the church in Thyatira in a threefold way. Remember, they were tolerating false teachers. Certain attributes of the Savior were appropriate to the message needed by this church. Her need was different from that of Ephesus and Smyrna. (1) The Lord Jesus first presented Himself as the Son of God. Something had intruded in this church that called for this emphasis. False doctrine always usurps the place of Jesus Christ. (2) The second of the threefold ways the Lord presented Himself to the church in Thyatira was that His eyes were like a flame of fire. This speaks of judgment. All things are open to Christ's eyes: *Neither is there any creature that is not manifest in his sight: but all things are naked and opened unto the eyes of him with whom we have to do, Heb. 4:13.* His eyes are as a flame of fire as He presently judges His own, knowing our innermost being *(Jer 17:9,10).* (3) The third of the threefold ways the Lord presented Himself to the church in Thyatira was with feet like brass. Brass is associated with judgment. This denotes judgment as Christ walks among the churches.

**E. The reason the revelation of Jesus Christ was to the church as it was, was because they *'hast a name that thou livest, and art dead'* and he said, *I have not found thy works perfect before God, 3:2.* The number 7 Spirits does not indicate 7 different Spirits or persons. The Holy Spirit is the third person in the Godhead. He is one, not seven. We find 7 characteristics of the Spirit in *Isa 11:2,* which was needed at this dying church. *And the spirit of the LORD shall rest upon him, the spirit of wisdom and understanding, the spirit of counsel and might, the spirit of knowledge and of the fear of the LORD.*

F. The church at Philadelphia, as well as Smyrna *received commendation. T*hey do not seem to be blamed for anything in doctrine, discipline, or manner of life. Of the Church of Philadelphia it is said, Thou *hast kept my word, and hast not denied my name.* Three attributes of Jesus are emphasized in the salutation— . . . . It means that which has not only the name, **'I am the truth'** but the real nature corresponding with the name . . . . .

Holiness is God's chief attribute. The holiness of God is Himself. It is the beauty of all of God's other attributes. He is holy in His omnipotence, omniscience, power, love, grace, and justice. One simple definition of holiness is self-affirming purity. A Christian's holiness is not holiness of equality but of similitude. Holiness has more than a negative quality. It is positive virtue. *2 Cor 5:21 For he hath made him to be sin for us, who knew no sin; that we might be made the righteousness of God in him.* It is not our own righteousness--*Phil 3:9 And be found in him, not having mine own righteousness, which is of the law, but that which is through the faith of Christ, the righteousness which is of God by faith.* Next Jesus says He *'true'.* It means that which has not only the name, *'I am the truth'* but the real nature corresponding with the name—real, true, or genuine. Jesus Christ *has the key of David.* He is the keeper of the key. The key of David has a wider application than simply the coming kingdom. The Lord

Jesus is now using the key on behalf of His people. No man or group of men hold the key of Christian service. Since God is absolutely sovereign and holds the key in His hand. He opens and closes doors. When He opens a door, no man can close it. Those who have the *Philadelphian* characteristics will not be stopped in their service or testimony for Christ, although they have no human influence or support and no human organization to promote success. God's man is not dependent on any religious talent scouts. A man's ministry cannot be evaluated by materialistic standards. As I said earlier there were two, namely, Smyrna and Philadelphia, who received commendation. The Lord opens doors that none can close to those who spend their time showing themselves approved unto God.

G. How Christ reveals Himself to the Laodiceans was very appropriate for their condition. Paul had a great concern for this church 25 years before the letter of Revelation was written to them. *Col 2:1 For I would that ye knew what great conflict I have for you, and for them at Laodicea, and for as many as have not seen my face in the flesh.* The church in Laodicea needed the lessons taught in the three characteristics in which the Lord presented Himself to her in the salutation: (1) As to the eternal, He is *the Amen.* He is the One in whom the purpose of God is fulfilled. (2) As to the external. He is *the faithful and true witness.* This has to do with the objective revelation of the mind of God given to His people. He is the witness of the Father. (3) As to the internal, He is the source of the very creation of God. He is the source of our creation—the new birth *(2 Cor.5:17).* These three fundamental truths were lacking among the

Laodiceans. They did not take Jesus Christ as the last Word. They were not believing He was the faithful and true witness, and *the beginning of the creation.*

I have given you the revelations (salutations) to the 7 churches. As I said earlier there were two, namely, *Smyrna* and *Philadelphia,* who *received commendation.* Two of them, namely, *Sardis* and *Laodicea,* are *censured.* Of the Church of Sardis it is said, *'Thou hast a name that thou livest, and thou art dead.'* Of the Church of Laodicea, *'I know thy works, that thou art neither cold nor hot: I would thou wert cold or hot.'* Three others are both *praised and blamed.* Those written to Ephesus, Pergamos, and Thyatira contain mingled censure and commendation. In some respects they deserve the one, and in some the other. In three cases, however, the praise precedes the blame, as Paul in his Epistles shows that it was more grateful to commend than to reprove.

How has the revelation of Jesus Christ come in your life? As we look at these churches more thoroughly in the coming weeks allow God to reveal Himself to you, both in commendation, as well as condemnation. If you have *left thy first love. Remember therefore from whence thou art fallen, and repent, and do the first works; or else I will come unto thee quickly, and will remove thy candle-stick out of his place, except thou repent, Rev 2:4, 5.*

This is one of 16 messages from the 'Seven Churches in Revelation' series, these messages are available on the 'Monitor Messages' CD.

A Mind to Work
Neh.4:1-6

¹ But it came to pass, that when Sanballat heard that we builded the wall, he was wroth, and took great indignation, and mocked the Jews.
² And he spake before his brethren and the army of Samaria, and said, What do these feeble Jews? will they fortify themselves? will they sacrifice? will they make an end in a day? will they revive the stones out of the heaps of the rubbish which are burned?
³ Now Tobiah the Ammonite *was* by him, and he said, Even that which they build, if a fox go up, he shall even break down their stone wall.
⁴ Hear, O our God; for we are despised: and turn their reproach upon their own head, and give them for a prey in the land of captivity:
⁵ And cover not their iniquity, and let not their sin be blotted out from before thee: for they have provoked *thee* to anger before the builders.
⁶ So built we the wall; and all the wall was joined together unto the half thereof: for the people had a mind to work.

In the previous message from *Neh.3* I gave some of the ones who worked with Nehemiah in rebuilding the wall around Jerusalem. He had a well-organized plan, as he assigned portions of the wall near their homes when possible. The first message in this series was on the leadership qualities of Nehemiah, as I encouraged you to *Follow the Leader.* Some of them were so eager they took on more than the work assigned them. Unfortunately, there were some who *'put not their necks to the work of their Lord,' Neh 3:5.* [The footnote in my Bible says they *'would not apply themselves to the work of the Lord.']* It is obvious that some had to take on extra work to get the job done. Pastors are always glad there are those who will see what needs to be done and do it, when others slack off. Though you sent out the postcards with the theme of our campaign on them, you may not have looked closely at the graphic of the broken down walls and the gates *on the back of bulletin.* [*Sending it with 2003 Stewardship Promotions]* I want you to look at what Nehemiah saw when he *went out by night by the gate of the valley, and viewed the walls of Jerusalem, which were broken down, and the gates thereof were consumed with fire, Neh 2:13.* Nehemiah had one task that God called him to do, and that was to rebuild a wall around Jerusalem. That doesn't sound too spiritual, but it was God's will for His life. Look at the picture, do you see why Sanballat mocked and said, *. . will they revive the stones out of the heaps of the rubbish which are burned?* Do you understand why some got discouraged? *Judah said, The strength of the bearers of burdens is decayed, and there is much rubbish; so that we are not able to build* *the wall, Neh 4:10.* In spite of all the opposition by their enemies and those who didn't do their part it tells us *all the wall was joined together unto the half thereof (v.6).* The display on the wall illustrates the portions of the wall assigned to each group who helped in rebuilding the walls. At this point of time the wall was half way up. It tells us in *v.7* that *the walls of Jerusalem were made up, and that the breaches began to be stopped.*

My message *'A Mind to Work,'* is a message of commendation to those of you who've attended faithfully all the services of the church and worked diligently in trying to get others in our services and help build the walls of our *'Arise and Build'* campaign display. But it is a message of admonition to any who have *'not applied themselves to the work of the Lord'* and have not done what you could have done.

The devotion in the bulletin is entitled, *'Praying, Working, and Watching.'* It starts out: *We cannot do without prayer if we are in God's work, nor should we allow prayer to become a substitute for work.* In the previous messages I have said quite a bit about the importance of prayer, not only in their rebuild-ing the wall, but also if we are to do the work of building the church. But do not forget the importance of work. *V.6, So built we the wall; and all the wall was joined together unto the half thereof: for the people had a mind to work.* Some may talk a good talk, but it takes a *'mind to work.' Prov 14:23, In all labour there is profit: but the talk of the lips tendeth only to penury* [poverty]. There are some who are sluggards who will say, *'I'm going to get a job making $50,000 a year,'* but their *lips tendeth* *only to penury* for the verse tells there must be labor to be profit. They are like the one who said, *'I'm not afraid of work, I can lay down and go to sleep by it anytime.'* Some no doubt talked a good talk saying, *We're going to get our part of the wall built before anyone else,* but then the rubbish got in the way, or they became discouraged. Before Nehemiah even started building the wall, the enemies taunted and mocked him, listen to his reply, *'then I answered them, and said unto them, The God of heaven, he will prosper us; therefore we his servants will arise and build, (2:20).*

In order to *'arise'* it is going to take an effort, but if we ever *'build'* it is going to take work—a lot of work! It is going to be inconvenient sometimes to come to church and to do a work for God. As I said in a previous message, that if you are doing a work for God there will be opposition, there will be those who will try to discourage you when they burn out or the rubbish is in the way-- *strength of the bearers of burdens is decayed, and there is much rubbish (v.10).* Some will keep on repeating the same old song of fear and discourage-ment *(v.12).* If you have no opposition, then maybe you are not working for the Lord like you ought to working. I read earlier *Prov 14:23, In all labour there is profit.* If you really start living for the Lord and doing what you can, there will be profit, not only in your life, but also the life of the church. However, if we sit on the *'seat of do nothing'* and talk about how the church ought to reach people—the talk by itself *tendeth only to penury* [poverty].

Nehemiah could have sat there in Persia and talked about how the walls needed to be rebuilt and the gates repaired in Jerusalem and it would never have happened. But he became concerned, and you know what happened—in only 52 days they rebuilt the wall. Another significant thing is everyone was assigned their work on the wall—so it is with the work of the church. The Holy Spirit has given each one a gift or gifts to be used in church ministries. *But all these worketh that one and the selfsame Spirit, dividing [assigning] to every man severally [individually] as he will, 1 Cor 12:11.*

How could those listed in *Neh.3* complete the building of the wall in 52 days? The answer is given in *Neh. 4:6, So built we the wall; and all the wall was joined together unto the half thereof: for the people had a mind to work.* How can we ever build up our church? The very same way! *Have a mind to work.* Do you want to see our church *'built up'* in the coming days? If you do, then I challenge you to *'arise and build.'* That means work! I looked up the word *'work'* in Strong's Con. and it was no surprise to me that the word is found 19 times in *Nehemiah* and 16 of those times are in the first 7 chapters.

Do you have a mind to work, or are you unemployed in the work of the Lord?

Most of the news we hear in our day is not good news, but a few days ago there was the good news that unemployment was down. I believe it would be a lot lower if some of those on the welfare rolls who are able to work would be forced to go back to work. It is a tragic thing to be able to work and want to work and be unemployed. But I'll tell you something which is even more tragic is when only 5% of born again Christians ever lead anyone to Christ! I'm not going to put you on the spot, but if I asked for a show of hands of those who have personally lead someone to the Lord only a few hands would go up. I am asking the question, *'Are You Unemployed?'* I am not talking now about your secular job, but I'm talking about something that is far more important than any secular job, than any amount of salary, than any fringe benefits, than any retirement plan, than the best job represented here this morning. I preached here some time ago using the text-***Psa.142:4, I looked on my right hand, and beheld, but there was no man that would know me: refuge failed me; no man cared for my soul.*** I still say as I said in that message: *We need to learn as never before what it is to care for souls, that it is every Christian's responsibility to care for souls and there are dire consequences, not only for the unsaved, but for you as well, if you don't care for souls.* ***(Ezek 3:17-21)*** I preached that message from ***Psa.142:4 i***n one church I was trying out at that was looking for a pastor and found that very few people were working for Jesus, they were unemployed, as far as God's work was concerned. I was at one church that had 2 busses and a van which could be running every Sunday yet only one of those busses was running and the driver was the S. S. Supt, who is also a deacon, who is also a S. S. teacher, who also had youth activities provided for the young people. That church at one time was averaging over 300, and they were averaging in the 50s when I was there. You say, what happened? The board when I met with them, admitted they had let up on evangelism, follow-up, caring for new converts and caring for one another. After meeting with the board, we had an open question and answer session with the people which I always request when I candidate for a church. When the question came up on church growth I answered them as candidly as I could and told them that prayer was the most important thing, I told them their personal concern and not a new pastor would bring about growth. I told the S. S. teachers and leaders that their concern didn't stop with prayer and teaching a S. S. class, but if they expected the classes to grow they must have activities; become more personally acquainted with the home situations; show their concern. I mean we covered every conceivable area of a pastor's responsibility down to dress standards at church activities, in public and even in the home. I told them the same thing I would tell you, if you asked the same questions. You say, Preacher, did you get the church? Obviously not! When I was looking for a new pastorate I was not politicking and I didn't sugar-coat the messages, as I have known some preachers to do in order to get a church when they go to other churches.

I'm going to preach what people need to hear, if I have to make nursing homes and jails my congregation. By the way, if you are unemployed for the Lord and have determined that you are going to remain so, this message will not tickle your ears. But if you unemployed for Jesus and will allow the Holy Spirit to speak to your heart and get some things settled this morning, this could be one of the most blessed services you have ever been in your life.

I believe the Lord's directed me to preach this topical message, *'A Mind to Work.'* I want to say again how I appreciate the prayers, work and effort that many have put into our enlargement campaign. However, if you have not done all you could do, then this message is primarily for you. There are 2 passages I want to share with you: *John 4:35,36; Luke 10:1-3.* Pay special attention to *v.2, The harvest truly is great, but the labourers are few: pray ye therefore the Lord of the harvest, that he would send forth labourers into his harvest.*

Are you unemployed? If you are, I want to show you how you can find a job this morning. *John 4:35, Say not ye, There are yet four months, and then cometh harvest? behold, I say unto you, Lift up your eyes, and look on the fields; for they are white already to harvest.* But our text says, *The harvest truly is great, but the labourers are few. Laborers are few.* They were few in Jesus' day and they are few today. Compared to laborers, the church goers are many, the churches are many, but laborers are few. Why is there such an unemployment problem in the church. Why does this situation persist year after year, decade after decade, century after century? Why are there never enough laborers? There are 5 basic reasons why you may be unemployed

I. First, if the devil wants to attack the foremost strategic element in revival and evangelization, where do you think he strikes? Where does he concentrate his efforts? Try to imagine an impact in a community of a church if every member was a spiritually qualified, separated, dedicated laborer, totally given over to Christ and His cause. What if the work of the church was not being handled by just the preacher and a few more. We need people whose greatest desire is to discover and fulfill God's will for their lives-laborers who upon leaving the church each Sunday go out into the world with the consuming desire to know Christ and make Him known. We know that the results of such a laboring force would be staggering. The devil knows that too and that is where he concentrates his efforts. Is that why you are unemployed this morning? Do you want as your greatest desire to discover and fulfill God's will for your life-here is how you do it-**Rom.12:1,2.** Have you done that?

II. Another reason for the church's unemployment problem—the reason why laborers are few, is found in the nature of the term itself-'*laborer.*' There is something unpleasant in the idea of being a laborer. By nature we would rather be a supervisor, manager, director, anything but a common laborer! That is exactly the meaning of the word that Jesus uses—a field hand, agricultural worker, one who works for hire. How degrading it is for some people to see themselves as nothing but field hands in the harvest! Humanly speaking, a common laborer is the last thing we want to be. Hey, if it wasn't for the common laborers on the farms in America you wouldn't be eating for long. If you think Russia, or any other country would send us their wheat and food if there was a famine like we have over the years ago, you better have another think coming. As I consider my own background, I am thankful for the days I spent in the hot dusty fields on a Bollinger County farm, putting up hay and milking the cows and planting and cultivating corn with a team of horses, so on. Admittedly it was hot, hard, dirty work, but there is something noble in that, and vitally important. The world does not get fed unless the field hand does his work. Somebody must harvest the crop. When the wheat grain was ripe it had to be brought in to the threshing machine and when the corn was ready it had to be picked. There's nothing humiliating about being one who performs such labor.

Are you unemployed? Do you have a mind to work? Are you afraid of work? Are you ready to dedicate yourself to the task that God has for you to do? He has a work to do for every believer. He prepares your tomorrows and when you by neglect fall into sin he even then *'makes a way to escape' (1 Cor 10:13).* He has a work to do thru every believer. You must let God work in you, for you, but you must let God work through you! If you ever amount to anything for Christ and His church you must work. God's work doesn't depend on preachers and paid staffs. It is my responsibility to get you in your work of the ministry *(Eph.4:11,12).* That is why I preach this message, if you are unemployed, get a mind work! There's plenty to do! *'The fields are white already to harvest!'* You may not like the word *'labor.'* Do you shy away because you know a laborer has it tough. Are you ready to dedicate yourself to the task, or are you going to shy away from being an ordinary field hand in the Kingdom of God. Do you feel that such a ministry is below your station in life? If so, remember this: Jesus was a laborer. He said, *I must work the works of him that sent me, while it is day: the night cometh, when no man can work, John 9:4.*

III. Another reason why many are unemployed for Jesus is because of short-sightedness. Although they see the cost and the labor involved, they fail to see the rewards. *Where there is no vision the people perish Prov 29:18.* I preach a message on nearsightedness [spiritual myopia]. Myopia, medically speaking, is a condition in which the visual images come to a focus in front of the retina of the eye because of defects in the refractive media of the eye, or a condition of abnormal length of the eyeball resulting in defective vision of distant objects---called nearsightedness, or short-sightedness. The spiritual shortsighted--myopic--person is one who closes his eyes and only sees what he wants to see. Man being the sinner that he is, only sees himself and his self-centeredness will show up in his lack of concern for others. It is a play on words, a my-opic person only sees *'I--me--mine--myself.'* They make every effort to *'look out for #1'* at all cost. That is humanism, a philosophy that pervades our society and is promoted by education, entertainment, economics, and every part of life. Humanism didn't begin with John Dewey in education; it began when mankind fell into sin in *Gen.3.*

How many of you had a vision, and I'm not talking about what some of the visions that some televangelists claim to see, but how many had a vision for this campaign of some labor you performed over the past weeks? I know that some of you had a vision of seeing some of your loved ones saved. Are you just seeing the cost of laboring for the Lord without a vision? Are you one who wants an instantaneous, costless, painless revival and all the benefits of revival at little or no cost? Do you want gain without pain, healing without surgery, joy without mourning? You do if don't have a mind to work! We must remember that the cost is high for anything that is truly valuable. A new Mercedes costs more than a 10 yr old Ford. But when you own one, you have something that will last. So it is with a laborer. Laborers are invaluable, indispensable and they are irreplaceable in God's great plan. Are you unemployed because you are short-sighted and have no vision. *'Lift up your eyes and look on the fields; for they are white already to harvest.'* Do you have spiritual myopia? Open your eyes, there is work to do!

IV. The fourth reason most people are unemployed is prayerlessness. I could put you on the spot now and ask how many of you prayed for some particular person to be in this service and be saved this morning? I'm not asking if you prayed for that person this week; I'm asking if you prayed they would be saved in this service?

Our text says we are to pray *for laborers into His harvest.* The very reason most people don't pray such a prayer is because they know that the Lord will probably say to them as He did to the 70: *Go your ways: behold, I send you forth as lambs among wolves, Luke 10:3.* Do you pray for laborers? Most people don't because they know the Lord will tell them to go themselves. Rather than pray, you worry and may fret because the church fails to grow. Rather to pray for the Sunday School and do all you can to see your class grow, you come expecting a handful to show up. Rather than witnessing, you soothe your conscience by saying the preacher and others can do the work of the ministry. Why don't you start praying to the Lord of the harvest?

V. The fifth and final reason for unemployment in Christ's church is not so easy to explain, but here goes: laborers are few because the majority of the Christian world does not even realize there is such a class of people. They know there are new converts. They know of disciples. They know there are Christian workers, missionaries, preachers, Christian leaders, but laborers are an unknown entity and are completely overlooked by most Christians. They fail to realize that the *'Great Commission'* is to all believers. *Mark 16:15 And he said unto them, Go ye into all the world, and preach the gospel to every creature.*

Are you unemployed? Do you have a mind to work? Are you not working for Jesus? All are called-- *John 15:16, Ye have not chosen me, but I have chosen you, and ordained you, that ye should go and bring forth fruit, and that your fruit should remain: that whatsoever ye shall ask of the Father in my name, he may give it you.* Few will follow—*The laborers are few, Lk.10:2.*

All may be saved *(John 3:16).* Few will be saved-*Enter ye in at the strait gate: for wide is the gate, and broad is the way, that leadeth to destruction, and many there be which go in there at: because strait is the gate, and narrow is the way, which leadeth unto life, and few there be that find it, Mat 7: 13,14.* The call is to all— both to follow and be saved. Are you one of the few following, or you one of the many unsaved?

To Christians I ask you—do you have a mind to work? If you are unemployed for Jesus, no doubt its one or more of these reasons: 1) you have not dedicated your body to God; 2) you don't want to labor-afraid of work; 3) you have no vision; 4) you don't pray as you should; or 5) you may be one of those up until this message didn't realize the work of the ministry is for everyone.

Whatever the reason might be, you need to come this morning and say by your coming that you are ready to get to work for the Lord.

This is one of 12 messages from the 'Nehemiah Messages' series, these messages are available on the 'Monitor Messages' CD.

Is Fasting Scriptural?
Matt. 6:16-18

¹⁶ *Moreover when ye fast, be not, as the hypocrites, of a sad countenance: for they disfigure their faces, that they may appear unto men to fast. Verily I say unto you, They have their reward.*
¹⁷ *But thou, when thou fastest, anoint thine head, and wash thy face;*
¹⁸ *That thou appear not unto men to fast, but unto thy Father which is in secret: and thy Father, which seeth in secret, shall reward thee openly.*

We must take the Sermon on the Mount as it comes, and here is the question of fasting confronting us, therefore, we must consider it. *How many have ever heard a message just on fasting?* In earlier messages we have looked at the religious practices of almsgiving and prayer, and now we consider fasting. As mentioned in an earlier message, these practices occupy a conspicuous place in all leading religions that depend upon a works salvation.

The Koran, holy book of the Muslims, teaches that prayer, alms and fasting are the chief duties of man. The Roman Catholic Church also stresses these as duties of their adherents. Because of this Protestants have gone to the other extreme and seldom or never fast. Christ once again shows that mere religious acts are worthless in the sight of God, who sees the heart. There may be a prolonged abstinence from food, and yet no fasting in the Scriptural sense. One may observe a weekly fast, and observe it strictly, and yet not fast at all if there is no expression of sorrow of the soul. The mere non-partaking of food is not fasting, any more than the moving of the lips is prayer.

There are several questions I want to answer in this message concerning fast-ing: *What is fasting?* Then we'll look at the questions: *Is fasting Scriptural? Should it be practiced and preached today? What are the benefits of fasting?* And finally, *what are the dangers of fasting?*

I. What is fasting? Dieting is not fasting! Going on a hunger strike is not fasting. Just simply doing without food is not fasting. *Fasting is denying oneself of normal sustenance for the express purpose of drawing closer to God.* I believe true fasting is always accompanied by a deep burdened soul. Illus: I have seen my mother being so engaged in prayer and under such a burden for me and my brother Harry until no thought was given to food— this is true fasting, although it is referred to as being under a burden for lost loved ones—that is true fasting. The Old Testament standard of fasting included the following: Strict abstinence from food; humble confession of sins to God; earnest seeking of God's face—

this often included sackcloth and ashes--**Dan 9:3, And I set my face unto the Lord God, to seek by prayer and supplications, with fasting, and sackcloth, and ashes;** also included true intercession for themselves and others; giving alms to the poor; and living as one prayed and vowed. Baker's Dictionary of Theology says *"fasting signifies deprivation of food, normally as deliberately undertaken for a religious purpose"* and does gives several Scriptures, which leads to the question . . .

II. Is fasting Scriptural? You may search the Mosaic Law and you will find that fasting is not found in the Pentateuch. Fasting within the Jewish religion was on a voluntary basis, not a legal act. But even so, there is evidence in both the Old and New Testament to say it is Scriptural.

This voluntary discipline was observed during public calamities--**2 Sam 1:12, And they mourned, and wept, and fasted until even, for Saul, and for Jonathan his son, and for the people of the LORD, and for the house of Israel; because they were fallen by the sword.** Private sorrow and concern--**2 Sam 12:16, David therefore besought God for the child; and David fasted, and went in, and lay all night upon the earth.** As an act of worship--**Luke 2:37, And she was a widow of about fourscore and four years, which departed not from the temple, but served God with fastings and prayers night and day.** To know the mind of God--**Acts 13:2,3, As they ministered to the Lord, and fasted, the Holy Ghost said, Separate me Barnabas and Saul for the work whereunto I have called them. And when they had fasted and prayed, and laid their hands on them, they sent them away.** Presbytery ordinations--**Acts 14:23,**

And when they had ordained them elders in every church, and had prayed with fasting, they commended them to the Lord, on whom they believed. Scriptural based incidents of fasting reveal its observance accompanied by prayer, as I read earlier--*Dan 9:3, And I set my face unto the Lord God, to seek by prayer and supplications, with fasting, and sackcloth, and ashes;* by reading of Scriptures--*Jer 36:6, Therefore go thou, and read in the roll, which thou hast written from my mouth, the words of the LORD in the ears of the people in the LORD'S house upon the fasting day: and also thou shalt read them in the ears of all Judah that come out of their cities;* repentance--*Neh 9:1,2, Now in the twenty and fourth day of this month the children of Israel were assembled with fasting, and with sackclothes, and earth upon them. And the seed of Israel separated themselves from all strangers, and stood and confessed their sins, and the iniquities of their fathers;* and bereavement--*2 Sam 12:21,22, Then said his servants unto him, What thing is this that thou hast done? thou didst fast and weep for the child, while it was alive; but when the child was dead, thou didst rise and eat bread. And he said, While the child was yet alive, I fasted and wept: for I said, Who can tell whether GOD will be gracious to me, that the child may live?*

III. Should fasting be preached and practiced today? It seems that Jesus in *v.16* recognizes fasting as an established practice. He did not say, *"If you fast"*, but *"when ye fast"*, so even though He did not teach fasting directly, He certainly taught it indirectly. He Himself fasted for forty days and nights when He was in the wilderness being tempted by the devil.. We read where the New Testament church sent out Paul and Barnabas only after a period of fasting and prayer. Paul in referring to himself in *2 Cor.11:27* talks about his being *"in fastings often".* It was clearly something that was a regular part of his life.

The saints of God in all ages . . . .and in all places have not only believed in fasting, they have practiced it. It was true of the Protestant Reformers, it was certainly true of the Charles and John Wesley, and George Whitefield.

I think the question, *Should fasting be practiced today? C*an be answered affirmatively by the Scripture references given and by the effect of those who practiced it in church history. I think it should also be preached and practiced because of the benefits derived from fasting, which is the next question . . .

IV. What are the benefits of fasting? 11 distinct blessings are seen in *Isa.58.*

A. Personal benefits: *Isa 58:6 Is not this the fast that I have chosen? to loose the bands of wickedness, to undo the heavy burdens, and to let the oppressed go free, and that ye break every yoke?*

1. The resulting activity of the one fasting:
a. Personal light shall break forth—understanding-- *Isa 58:8, Then shall thy light break forth as the morning;*
b. Personal health shall spring forth--*thine health shall spring forth speedily;*

c. Personal righteousness shall go forth—cleansing-- *thy righteousness shall go before thee;*

d. Personal providential care--*the glory of the LORD shall be thy reward.*

e. The Lord answering our prayers--*Isa 58:9a, Then shalt thou call, and the LORD shall answer; thou shalt cry, and he shall say, Here I am.*

2. The resulting activity on the part of God--*Isa 58:11,12, And the LORD shall guide thee continually, and satisfy thy soul in drought, and make fat thy bones: and thou shalt be like a watered garden, and like a spring of water, whose waters fail not. And they that shall be of thee shall build the old waste places: thou shalt raise up the foundations of many generations; and thou shalt be called, The repairer of the breach, The restorer of paths to dwell in.*

a. He will *guide thee continually.*

b. He will satisfy your soul *in drought,* in times of distress.

c. He will supply your needs-- *make fat thy bones.*

d. He will produce fruit through you--*like a watered garden.*

e. You will have fullness of the Spirit--*like a spring of water, whose waters fail not. John 7:38, 39a, He that believeth on me, as the scripture hath said, out of his belly shall flow rivers of living water. But this spake he of the Spirit, which they that believe on him should receive.*

f. God's 11th promise to those who fast is threefold to *they that shall be of thee shall build the old waste places, Isa 58:12:* (1) *thou shalt raise up the foundations of many generations;* (2) *thou shalt be called, The repairer of the breach,* and (3) *the restorer of paths to dwell in.* All of these are needed in the church of our day. The cry needs to be heard in our day, *Jer 6:16, Thus saith the LORD, Stand ye in the ways, and see, and ask for the old paths, where is the good way, and walk therein, and ye shall find rest for your souls.*

Seeing the results of fasting—the pledged results, one should have no problem is saying that fasting should be practiced by believers in our day!

B. The corporate benefits in fasting with others:

1. Brings unity of purpose to a nation, or a group of believers. This past Thursday was a *National Day of Prayer.* I've often wondered how effective a national day of prayer is in our country, when you see Christ-rejecting, God-denying, Scripture-rejecting liberals participating. Now I am not saying we should not have a day set aside to pray for our country, but you know as well as I do that many of the prayers prayed Thursday did not reach the Throne of God, for it says in *John 9:31, Now we know that God heareth not sinners: but if any man be a worshipper of God, and doeth his will, him he heareth.*

2. Creates a unified burden for whatever the fast is called--a corporate benefit.

3. It will produce results—*(Jonah 3:5-10)*

V. **What are the dangers of fasting?** There are several wrong ways to fast:

A. Asceticism or legalism. Asceticism comes from a Greek word which means exercise or training, and denotes the practice of self-discipline, more particularly in relation to the body. The Gnostics, a pagan belief during New Testament times, believed that the physical part of man is essentially evil and therefore must be renounced. Roman Catholicism have rules of asceticism on their insistence upon a celibate clergy, not allowing priests to marry. (There is more to the story of the priests and nuns being married to the church than has been revealed.) The season of lent is also a time of ascetic practice for Catholics, and some other religions, for a supposedly higher level of Christian life, and acquires merit for Catholics in their bid to escape purgatory.

B. Susceptibility to demon influence. *1 Tim 4:1-3, Now the Spirit speaketh expressly, that in the latter times some shall depart from the faith, giving heed to seducing spirits, and doctrines of devils; speaking lies in hypocrisy; having their conscience seared with a hot iron; forbidding to marry, and commanding to abstain from meats, which God hath created to be received with thanksgiving of them which believe and know the truth.*

C. False piety, which Christ makes reference to in *Mat 6:16, Moreover when ye fast, be not, as the hypocrites, of a sad countenance: for they disfigure their faces, that they may appear unto men to fast..* In *Lk. 18:12* the publican said, *"I fast twice in the week."* (that is one hundred four times a year)

It is possible to take a perfectly good thing and abuse it, as we look again in *Isa 58, fasting for God to see, v.3a, Wherefore have we fasted, say they, and thou seest not? To merely abstain from food, v.3b, wherefore have we afflicted our soul, and thou takest no knowledge? For something to boast about, v. 3c, Behold, in the day of your fast ye find pleasure.* To oppress employees, *and exact all your labours.* The word *exact* means *"to drive(a workman, a debt-or, an army); by impl. to tax, harass, tyrannize:--distress"*--Strong'sCon. In the Iran hostage crisis 52 American diplomats and citizens were held hostage for 444 days (November 4, 1979, to January 20, 1981), by a group of Muslims When they were being held hostage in Iran I sent a letter to their captors who were fasting at that time and included these verses in *Isa 58:4,5, Behold, ye fast for strife and debate, and to smite with the fist of wickedness: ye shall not fast as ye do this day, to make your voice to be heard on high. Is it such a fast that I have chosen? a day for a man to afflict his soul? is it to bow down his head as a bulrush, and to spread sackcloth and ashes under him?* They were fasting for strife, smiting with a wicked fist, trying to obligate their God Allah to hear their prayers, sitting in sackcloth and ashes, and God says, *wilt thou call this a fast, and an acceptable day to the LORD?*

D. I feel there is also a danger for some to practice fasting when their health is not good. *Col 2:21-23, (Touch not; taste not; handle not; which all are to perish with the using;) after the commandments and doctrines of men? Which things have indeed a show of wisdom in will worship, and humility, and neglecting of the body; not in any honour to the satisfying of the flesh.* More could be said of this verse of neglecting the body.

I believe that fasting is Scriptural, it should be practiced individually as well as corporately, but we must be on guard concerning the dangers associated with it. One of the reasons I would never have you pledge that you will fast when we are praying and fasting for a particular burden or need of the church, is that it could produce a false piety. This is not to say we should never call for a time of fasting and prayer, but I don't want to know if you are fasting with others. God knows whether you are or not, and that is what counts.

Never fast with the thought of obligating God and think because I fast the Lord is forced to bless me or make me a blessing. Just because we fast, pray, or tithe, we cannot obligate God and make Him our servant. We should never fast as a means of obtaining direct blessing; the value of fasting is indirect and not direct. *Why then should a Christian fast?* Because he feels impelled to do so for some spiritual reason, but it shouldn't be routine or mechanical, and should be prompted by the Holy Spirit. Perhaps this message will be used of the Holy Spirit to convict you about really getting serious with God concern-ing something you have been praying about. Jesus does indicate that some things require both prayer and fasting--**Mk 9:29, He said unto them, This kind can come forth by nothing, but by prayer _and fasting._**

This has not been an evangelistic message, but if you are here and expect the Lord to hear your prayers, then you must be a *"a worshipper of God." I* read earlier--**John 9:31, Now we know that God heareth not sinners:**

but if any man be a worshipper of God, and doeth his will, him he heareth. God will hear the sinner's prayer of repentance, for by praying such a prayer you do become *"a worshipper of God."* You're doing His will and the promise is *"him he heareth"* What is the will of God for every lost sinner? *1 Tim 2:4, Who will* [wills to] *have all men to be saved, and to come unto the knowledge of the truth.* I hope no one will put of salvation by not having Jesus as Lord, as I did numerous times, for it was only by His grace and longsuffering that I am not burning in hell right now. Sinner, He is not willing that you perish, but He wills that you come to repentance today-- *2 Pet 3:9.*

This is one of 55 messages from the 'Sermon on the Mount' series, all of these messages are available on the 'Monitor Messages' CD.

America and the 10 Commandments
Exo.20:3-17

3 Thou shalt have no other gods before me.

4 Thou shalt not make unto thee any graven image, or any likeness *of anything* that *is* in heaven above, or that *is* in the earth beneath, or that *is* in the water under the earth:

5 Thou shalt not bow down thyself to them, nor serve them: for I the LORD thy God *am* a jealous God, visiting the iniquity of the fathers upon the children unto the third and fourth *generation* of them that hate me;

6 And shewing mercy unto thousands of them that love me, and keep my commandments.

7 Thou shalt not take the name of the LORD thy God in vain; for the LORD will not hold him guiltless that taketh his name in vain.

8 Remember the sabbath day, to keep it holy.

9 Six days shalt thou labour, and do all thy work:

10 But the seventh day *is* the sabbath of the LORD thy God: *in it* thou shalt not do any work, thou, nor thy son, nor thy

daughter, thy manservant, nor thy maidservant, nor thy cattle, nor thy stranger that *is* within thy gates:

11 For *in* six days the LORD made heaven and earth, the sea, and all that in them *is*, and rested the seventh day: wherefore the LORD blessed the sabbath day, and hallowed it.

12 Honour thy father and thy mother: that thy days may be long upon the land which the LORD thy God giveth thee.

13 Thou shalt not kill.

14 Thou shalt not commit adultery.

15 Thou shalt not steal.

16 Thou shalt not bear false witness against thy neighbour.

17 Thou shalt not covet thy neighbour's house, thou shalt not covet thy neighbour's wife, nor his manservant, nor his maidservant, nor his ox, nor his ass, nor any thing that *is* thy neighbour's.

18 And all the people saw the thunderings, and the lightnings, and the noise of the trumpet, and the mountain smoking: and when the people saw *it*, they removed, and stood afar off.

19 And they said unto Moses, Speak thou with us, and we will hear: but let not God speak with us, lest we die.

20 And Moses said unto the people, Fear not: for God is come to prove you, and that his fear may be before your faces that ye sin not.

On this Independence Day weekend I feel it is appropriate to preach the mes-sage I am preaching today concerning *America and the 10 Commandments,* for it tells us in **Psa 9:17, The wicked shall be turned into hell, and all the nations that forget God.** I preached a message earlier entitled, *'The State of the Union,'* and I really believe that one of the things that has our nation in its present state is that we in America have forgotten the 10 Commandments.

In America we have those controlling our media who are trying to destroy the very principles our nation was founded upon. By media I mean not only TV, but radio, the printed page, and the music America is listening to. The Ten Commandments are no longer regarded as principles to live by and the ACLU and their cohorts wants to remove their engravings and display from all of our public places and court rooms. The sitcoms make a big joke out of more than one of the 10 Commandments; especially adultery.

One of those who is out to destroy our foundations as a nation is the media icon Ted Turner. I quote from the Plains Baptist Challenger, *Ted Turner with much fanfare, gave $1 billion to the UN. He won the 1990 Humanist of the Year award. He says 'heaven is going to be perfect, and I don't really want to be there.' He says 'Christianity has been unsuccessful after trying for 2000 years to solve the world's problems, so why don't we start over.' He complains that 'there is no amendment procedure to the Ten Commandments.' He recommends a new ten commandments, with the first one beginning, 'Love and respect the planet,' and the third one stating, 'Promise to have no more than two children or no more than one's nation suggests.' His eighth and tenth both give glory to the UN. Ted Turner said 'The Ten Commandments are out of date.' He said, '...I don't know if [prohibiting] adultery should be one of them,' and that Christian themselves are 'dummies.'* I know who the dummy is, don't you? For the

Bible tells us so in both *Psa 14:1* and *Psa 53:1 The fool hath said in his heart, There is no God. They are corrupt, they have done abominable works, there is none that doeth good.* Ted Turner is the kind of fool [dummy] that so many in America are being hoodwinked by. The deception has caused us as a nation to lose our mooring and now we are not only breaking just one of the Commandments but all of them, which I hope you will see in this message. We are warned in *James 2:10, For whosoever shall keep the whole law, and yet offend in one point, he is guilty of all.* James mentions the *'law'* ten times in his epistle, and in each case it is the moral law.

Easton's Bible Dictionary says, *The moral law, as revealed in the 10 Com-mandments is the revealed will of God as to human conduct, binding on all men to the end of time. It was proclaimed at Sinai. It is perfect (Ps. 19:7), it is perpetual (Matt. 5:17, 18), holy, and just, and good. (Rom. 7:12), and spiritual (Rom. 7:14), and exceeding broad (Ps. 119:96). Although binding on all, we are not under it as a covenant of works (Gal. 3:17).*

What about America and the 10 Commandments? Are we as a nation breaking any, or all, of the Commandments? This message is for you to be the judge as to what has happened in America. I am not asking you to believe what your preacher believes, but for you to be honest with God and yourself!

I. America and the 1st Commandment--Exo 20:3 Thou shalt have no other gods before me.

I ask you—is this commandment being broken in America, but even more important, is it being broken by you? I want these messages to be as practical as possible, that we not just look at the sins of others, but at our own sins. We know that in America there are many other gods being served. What are the gods that are prevalent in America? I think of the *'god of pleasure'* this includes not only the nightclubs and bars with their immoral shows; the race tracks of cars, horses and greyhounds; the casinos are the gods of many. Then there is the sports craze we have in America, where people talk more about their teams or individual sports figures than they ever talk about God. Camping, hunting and fishing are the gods of many, as they are out on the lakes or on the creek banks today rather than in the house of God. The amusement parks do a tremendous business on the weekends during the summer months, and sad to say there are 'Christians' who are at these places today. The word *'amuse'* means *made not muse, or think.* The word muse means 'to ponder, meditate, and reflect' and the letter 'a' negates the word. The god of amusement is being used by the devil to get people not thinking about God while they are out of church today. Now not all of the things I have mentioned are a sin in and of themselves, but they become a sin when you put them before God and they keep you out of church. ***Thou shalt have no other gods before me.***

Then there is the *'god of materialism'* that is also prevalent in America. God's blessing on America is being used in a negative sense when people are *'getting all they can'* and *'canning what they get.'* America needs to be told what God told Israel in ***Deu 8:18, But thou shalt remember the LORD thy God: for it is he that giveth thee power to get wealth.***

I could go on with the many gods in America that are distracting people from Who the Lord says He is right before giving the 10 Commandments in ***Exo 20: 2 I am the LORD thy God.*** The next commandment reveals the gods of many.

II. America and the 2nd Commandment. Exo 20:4,5, *Thou shalt not make unto thee any graven image . . Thou shalt not bow down thyself to them, nor serve them: for I the LORD thy God am a jealous God.* Now obviously we see many *'graven images'* in some of the world's religions; not only of Jesus, Mary and the saints, but we see in America, because of our expanding culture, the gods of the Hindus, the Buddhists, the Shinto's and other New Age gods. But the fact is, this commandment may be broken without a graven image, as many are bowing and serving other gods from their heart. The heart is what the Lord sees and He knows when we or anyone else is putting things before Him. You have never seen anyone with a statue of a dollar out in their yard who is living in a million or half-million dollar home. But you know that in all probability there is their graven image of that home with all its gardens, lakes and beautiful lawn. You especially know it is an image one serves when they are out there on Sunday morning grooming their image rather than being in church.

III. America and the 3rd Commandment. Exo 20:7, ***Thou shalt not take the name of the LORD thy God in vain.*** In the introduction I mentioned how the media has influenced us away from the 10 Commandments, and you can't sit down and watch most of the shows on TV for very long until you hear the name of the Lord in vain. And if it's not swearing it is *'corrupt communication as* it is called in *Eph 4:29,* or *'filthy communication as* it is called in *Col 3:8.* Some were talking recently how that when we were being raised that even filthy mouthed and cursing men would not cuss and say some four letter words around women and children, that many of our kids and women are using today.

There is another way that this commandment is being broken by many today, and it is not by their mouth but their life style. The word *'conversation'* in the Bible is properly translated *'behavior'* or *'lifestyle.'* One takes the name of the Lord in vain when they call themselves a *'Christian'* and are not *'Christ-like.'* What gets to me are people who will have on a tee-shirt with some Christian writing or symbols on it and they are running around half-naked.

IV. America and the 4th Commandment. Exo 20:8 ***Remember the sabbath day, to keep it holy.*** I'll have some more to say about the 4th Commandment when I get to it in this series of messages.

If you don't think America has desecrated the Lord's Day, which is the Christian Sabbath, then you have not opened your eyes. Some breaking of the other commandments happened more openly earlier in my life, but in the past few years we have seen the *'Blue Law'* made null and void as Walmart and other big companies out of greed want to stay open on Sundays so you can spend your money. Right now, when people ought to be in church, you can drive down by Walmart and you will see their lot packed with cars. Then you wait until about 12 noon and drive by the restaurants and you will see their lots packed with the cars of Christians. You ask any restaurant owner and they will tell you that if it were not for the *'church crowd'* they couldn't stay open on Sundays.

V. America and the 5ᵗʰ Commandment. Exo 20:12, ***Honour thy father and thy mother.*** We recently celebrated two holidays set aside to honor fathers and mothers—Mother's Day and Father's Day. But sad to say in America some do not even honor them on these days. In my previous pastorate we had a nursing home ministry at three homes. We would go there once a month and many of those we ministered to saw us more than they did their children. Now I am not against anyone putting their parents in a nursing home if they get to the point that they need such care; but I am against those who will put their parents in such a place and then forget all about them. This is another thing that has come about in my life time. The word *'nursing home'* wasn't in the vocabulary in Bollinger County when I was a child. Yes, it is sad that some parents do not deserve honor in our day as a result of infidelity, divorce, alcohol, drugs, abuse and other things, but the Bible tells us to honor them.

VI. America and the 6ᵗʰ Commandment. Exo 20:13, ***Thou shalt not kill.*** In America every 20 seconds an unborn baby is being murdered and we don't even know how many older people are being killed by euthanasia. It is murder when anyone takes the life of another by abortion or euthanasia. Here is where some show dishonor to their parents, as they don't want the doctor to prolong the lives of their parents. Don't misunderstand what I am saying, I am not for putting people on life support when it is obvious they have no hope of recovering. When we get to this commandment in the message series I want you to understand that many kill with their tongues the influence of others. I would rather you come and shoot me right now as I preach than for you to slander my name and kill my influence.

VII. America and the 7ᵗʰ Commandment. Exo 20:14, ***Thou shalt not commit adultery.*** I don't have to tell you how this Commandment is being broken in America. Many of us know those of our own family and friends who have been the victim of this sin, or committed it, and some are committing it right now. It tells you something about the *'Christianity'* in America when the divorce rate even among those who call themselves Christians is over 50%. But remember this is a commandment that is being broken by many in their heart, as I shared with you in a previous message when Christ said in the Sermon on the Mount, ***Mat 5:28, But I say unto you, That whosoever looketh on a woman to lust after her hath committed adultery with her already in his heart.*** Something could be said here about the immoral dress of women. Here again is where the *'god of pleasure,'* the entertainment media has many committing adultery in their heart by their eyes. God help us to make the commitment of the Psalmist in *Psa 101:3, I will set no wicked thing before mine eyes: I hate the work of them that turn aside; it shall not cleave to me.* As Job in *Job 31:1, I made a covenant with mine eyes; why then should I think upon a maid?*

VIII. America and the 8th Commandment. Exo 20:15,
Thou shalt not steal. American businesses have to figure a high percentage for the shoplifting that goes on in their stores. It would probably shock all of us to hear how many things are stolen by people from their employers. Stealing has become a com-mon practice with many in America. When I worked at Dow Chemical we had a hard time keeping 10 quart galvanized pails and big scoop shovels, as they were always having to order and replace them. You heard about the fellow who would go past the guard at the gate every night pushing a wheel barrow. He would have his lunch bucket and his coat thrown over his lunch bucket in the wheel barrow and the guard would always look under his coat and in the lunch bucket to see if he was stealing from the company. Come to find out he was stealing a wheel barrow every time he was being inspected by the guard.

IX. America and the 9th Commandment. Exo 20:16,
Thou shalt not bear false witness against thy neighbour. Because of our judicial system in America there are many serving time in prison that are innocent because of a false witness. Then there are some like O. J. Simpson who have influence and money, who are guilty and yet running around free. [*This was before O. J. was convicted*]. I am not upholding those who may have been

in the wrong place at the wrong time. You ask anyone who is in prison they are quick to make an excuse and will tell you why they don't deserve to be in prison. I have visited with some and I know what I am talking about. But you know that in America sometimes the innocent suffer as a result of the false witness against them. Bringing this down to us—gossip is false witnessing and that is one of the reasons I will not put up with it in the church, and I preached an annual message on gossip.

X. America and the 10ᵗʰ Commandment. Exo 20:17, *Thou shalt not covet.* One of the plagues in America is gambling, which has become a common practice in our day. It is another one of those sins that has destroyed and wrecked many homes. People always want something for nothing without having to work for it. I don't have a thing I didn't work for. What is sad is that many people who are on welfare spend what money they do have on gambling. They covet the money that other fools have spent hoping they too would be rich. Anyone who can't see the overwhelming odds of them ever winning anything are blinded with the sin of covetousness and greed.

I ask you again—Are we as a nation breaking any, or all, of the Commandments? This message is for you to be the judge as to what has happened in America. But the Bible tells us that we must judge ourselves when it comes to sin if our lives—***2 Cor 13:5, Examine yourselves, whether ye be in the faith; prove your own selves.*** Are you breaking the 10 Commandments? Do you have other gods? You may not have an image you are bowing down to, but who are you serving? Are you by your lifestyle taking His name in vain—claiming to be a Christian, but your life is not Christ-like? What do you do on Sunday? Is it a day of worship and rest, or are you following the world in desecrating His day? Do you show proper respect and honor to your parents? Do you kill others influence by your tongue? Do you commit adultery in your heart? Have you stolen or took that which wasn't yours? Do you bear false witness by gossiping? Do you covet what others have? ***Covetousness, which is idolatry, Col 3:5. Examine yourselves.*** You be your own judge today!

This is one of 20 messages from the 'Ten Commandment' series, these messages are available on the 'Monitor Messages' CD. It is also one of 38 messages on 'Godly Patriotism' on the 'Holidays and Special Services' CD which has 534 messages.

The Sounds of His Coming
1 Thess. 4:16

16 For the Lord himself shall descend from heaven with a shout, with the voice of the archangel, and with the trump of God: and the dead in Christ shall rise first:

My message is, *'The Sounds of His Coming.'* Our text says there will be the *shout of the Lord, the voice of the arch angel and the trump of God.* I will be saying some more about these 3 sounds of His 2nd Coming, but I want to say in the beginning of the message that it will be a personal return of the Lord--**the Lord himself shall descend from heaven**.

He will not send His angels to call the saints from the grave; He will return personally in His glorified body and here is what will happen to believers when He comes— *he shall change our vile body that it may be fashioned like unto his glorious body, Phil 3:21.* As sure as He personally ascended, just as sure *the Lord himself shall descend from heaven.* Remember message of the angels at His ascension--*Acts 1:9-11, And when He had spoken these things, while they beheld, He was taken up; and a cloud received Him out of their sight. And while they looked stedfastly toward heaven as he went up, behold, two men stood by them in white apparel; which also said, Ye men of Galilee, why stand ye gazing up into heaven? This same Jesus, which is taken up from you into heaven, shall so come in like manner as ye have seen him go into heaven.* He is coming in the clouds, just like He said He would--*1 Th 4:17, Then we which are alive and remain shall be caught up together with them in the clouds, to meet the Lord.* Agnostics will tell you the word 'rapture' is not in the Bible. From the Latin translation we get our word 'rapture,' which is the literal meaning *of 'caught up.'* The Latin word 'rapto' means 'to seize, to carry off'; and from it we get our English word 'rapture.' The words *caught up i*s a translation of the Greek word *harpazo* which means to 'snatch,' or 'seize,' and denotes a sudden violent taking away. The word pictures being 'swept off' into the air as by a tornado. Result of this sweeping away is that we meet the Lord in the air. Jesus said the way it would be in *Mat.24:40-42. The Lord himself shall descend from heaven,* not by proxy, or representatives; not by the ministry of angels, as in the Old Testament; nor by the ministers of the word, as under the Gospel dispensation; nor by His spirit; but in person, in His soul and body; in like manner as He went up to heaven He shall descend from there, visible, to be seen and heard by those who have the *'blessed hope'.* He will come down from the 3rd heaven, where he was carried up, into which he was received, and where He sits on the right hand of the Father as our mediator—*1 Tim 2:5, For there is one God, and one mediator between God and men, the man Christ Jesus.* He ascended bodily in His resurrection body, and He is still in that body and will return bodily. He will return personally and tells us in *John 14:3, And if I go and prepare a place for you, I will come again, and receive you unto myself; that where I am, there ye may be also.* Note He says, *I will come again.*

My message is, *'the sounds of His coming.'* Our text says there will be the *shout of the Lord, the voice of the arch angel and the trump of God.*

I. The Shout of the Lord. A *'shout'* will accompany Christ's descent. The noun translated *'shout'* means a *'shout of command'* and implies authority and urgency. Barnes says, The word used here does not elsewhere occur in the New Testament. It properly means a *'cry'* of excitement, or of urging on; an outcry, clamor, or shout, as of sailors at the oar; of soldiers rushing to battle; of a huntsman to his dogs. Robertson says it means to *order, command (military command). He will come as Conqueror.* What does He conquer? Death and the grave! *1 Cor 15:54-57, So when this corruptible shall have put on incorruption, and this mortal shall have put on immortality, then shall be brought to pass the saying that is written, Death is swallowed up in victory. O death, where is thy sting? O grave, where is thy victory? The sting of death is sin; and the strength of sin is the law. But thanks be to God, which giveth us the victory through our Lord Jesus Christ.* I heard a preacher say, the reason *'He cried with a loud voice,*

Lazarus, come forth,' in *John 11:43,* when Lazarus was raised from the dead, was to signify just Lazarus. Otherwise at the power of His command all of the dead would have been raised. Whether that's true or not, we do know the day is coming, and I believe soon, when the shout of Christ Himself, the mighty conqueror over death, awakens the bodies of the dead in Christ to immortal life. *John 5: 28,29a, Marvel not at this: for the hour is coming, in the all that are in the graves shall hear his voice, and shall come forth; they that have done good, unto the resurrection of life.*

The shout of the Lord Himself will be of great significance to those who are *'sleeping in Jesus'* who He will bring with Him for their new bodies, as well as those living who have **'Christ in you, the hope of glory,' Col 1:27.** The rapture does not seem to be a silent affair. It seems that a tremendous reverberating sound will encircle the earth. Some seem to think that the world will be unaware of the rapture, that the saints will silently slip away and the world will hardly note their absence. Others think that the rapture, as described, will as a truly *'noisy affair'* and will be heard by all. An intermediate position seems to be nearer the truth. The unsaved world will realize that something extraordinary and supernatural has taken place, but it does not necessarily follow they will understand the significance of the sound and realize exactly what has taken place. Remember, it tells us at the rapture, that those *'who received not the love of the truth, that they might be saved. And for this cause God shall send them strong delusion, that they should believe a lie,' 2 Th 2:10,11.* Let me assure you that the anti-christ will have an explanation and people probably now living who have rejected Christ's *love of the truth, that they might be saved,* will fall hook, line and sinker for his lies. How can this be? *God shall send them strong delusion, that they should believe a lie.* One commentary said, *'The world shall hear the shout of His coming, much as those who traveled with Saul on the road to Damascus, who heard the sound of the voice, but evidently did not articulate words, and who saw no man--Acts 9:7, And the men which journeyed with him stood speechless, hearing a voice, but seeing no man. Acts 22:9, And they that were with me saw indeed the light, and were afraid; but they heard not the voice of him that spake to me.* When a voice spoke to Jesus His last week on earth, all those present heard a sound but it was differently interpreted by various people. *John 12:28,29, Father, glorify thy name. Then came there a voice from heaven, saying, I have both glorified it, and will glorify it again. The people therefore, that stood by, and heard it, said that it thundered: others said, An angel spake to him.* Another sound heard:

II. The voice of the archangel. From *Dan.10:12-21* we learn a battle is going on between good and evil angels as they influence the affairs if men. It says of the archangel Michael--*Dan 10:21, But I will show thee that which is noted in the scripture of truth: and there is none that holdeth with me in these things, but Michael your prince.* The word *'archangel'* is only mentioned one other time in the New Testament, where it is directly associated with Michael--*Jude 9, Yet Michael the archangel, when contending with the devil he disputed about the body of Moses.* Whether or not there is more than one archangel cannot be categorically answered from Scripture. Michael is the only one referred to as an archangel, but the reference in **Dan 10:13** says, **Michael, <u>one</u> of the chief princes, came to help me.** Some say that Gabriel, the angel who interprets Daniel's vision and reveals prophecy to him, who also announced John the Baptist's and Jesus birth, and it does say of him, when he came to announce John's birth--**Luke 1:19, And the angel answering said unto him, I am Gabriel, that stand in the presence of God; and am sent to speak unto thee, and to show thee these glad tidings.** Some say that Lucifer was the third archangel before his fall and it does indicate that a third of the angels followed him in his rebellion against God in **Rev 12:4, And his tail drew the third part of the stars of heaven, and did cast them to the earth.** It does speak of the battle between the forces of evil and Michael in **Rev 12:7-9, And there was war in heaven: Michael and his angels fought against the dragon; and the dragon fought and his angels, and prevailed not; neither was their place found any more in heaven. And the great dragon was cast out, that old serpent, called the Devil, and Satan, which deceiveth the whole world: he was cast out into the earth, and his angels were cast out with him.** It seems reasonable that when Christ returns, He will be invading Satan's domain, as Satan is referred to as **'the prince of the power of the air,' Eph 2:2.** Remember when they came to arrest Jesus He said, **Mat 26: 53, Thinkest thou that I cannot now pray to my Father, and he shall presently give me more than twelve legions of angels?** Obviously Satan will resist Christ's effort to remove believers from his domain, so angelic forces will be called upon to resist the forces of

Satan as Christ removes the Church from the earth. Does this mean *'the voice of the archangel'* Michael will call for help?

III. Thirdly, there will be the sound of the trumpet of God. This denotes a trumpet belonging to God--*the trump of God.* This is a clear parallel to the *'last trump'* in *1 Cor.15:52* since both passages relate to the rapture of the church--*1 Cor 15:52,53, In a moment, in the twinkling of an eye, at the last trump: for the trumpet shall sound, and the dead shall be raised incorruptible, and we shall be changed. For this corruptible must put on incorruption, and this mortal must put on immortality.* Some confuse this with the trumpet call when Jesus comes back in power to rule and reign--*Mat 24:29-31, Immediately after the tribulation of those days shall the sun be darkened, and the moon shall not give her light, and the stars shall fall from heaven, and the powers of the heavens shall be shaken: and then shall appear the sign of the Son of man in heaven: and then shall all the tribes of the earth mourn, and they shall see the Son of man coming in the clouds of heaven with power and great glory. And he shall send his angels with a great sound of a trumpet, and they shall gather together his elect from the four winds, from one end of heaven to the other.* There is a similarity, as the blowing of a trumpet was used in gathering of the Lord's people, but there is a marked difference. The subjects being called are different: the call at the rapture is to the Church, and *Matt.24* portrays Jewish believers called after the great tribulation. The circumstances are different: at the rapture the trumpet is connected with the raising of the believing dead; there no mention is made of a resurrection, but is connected with a regathering of the elect Jews who have been scattered over the earth. The result is different: here the blowing of the trumpet results in the uniting of those who have died *'in the Lord'* and presently with Jesus and those who are *'alive and remain shall be caught up together with them in the clouds;* there in *Matt.24* it is living believers who are gathered from all parts of the earth at the command of the Lord Who has returned to earth in power and glory to rule and reign for a 1000 years.

This first part of the message are the sounds of His coming for believers, but does it have anything to say to those who are unbelievers, having never trusted Christ as Saviour?

IV. The sounds unbelievers will hear. I purposely did not read the last part of *John 5:28,29* earlier, for it says, *'Marvel not at this: for the hour is coming, in the which all that are in the graves shall hear his voice, and shall come forth; they that have done good, unto the resurrection of life; and they that have done evil, unto the resurrection of damnation'.* This resurrection of damnation is the *'second resurrection'* I preached about earlier. We saw from Scripture, that after the first resurrection, there will be 1000 years of torment in hell for the unbelievers before they are summoned by God to appear at the Great White Throne judgment. *Rev 20:5,6, But the rest of the dead lived not again until the thousand years were finished. This is the first resurrection. Blessed and holy is he that hath part in the first resurrection: on such the second death hath no power, but they shall be priests of God and of*

*Christ, and shall reign with him a thousand years. W*hile we who have been called by the last trumpet at the resurrection, and those gathered Jewish believers in Matt.24 are ruling and reigning with Christ, unbelievers will continue their existence in hell.

As noted earlier, there will be an explanation for the sounds of Christ's coming promoted by the anti-christ, and because of a God-sent delusion they will believe it, if they are left behind at the rapture. The voice of the angel they will be hearing, is the voice of the fallen angel Lucifer, who is a liar and a murderer. I thought it was very interesting that the verse preceding calling the devil a liar and murderer says, *Why do ye not understand my speech? even because ye cannot hear my word, John 8:43.* Unbelievers now are like the unbelievers then, in not hearing Him and it says, *Ye are of your father the devil, and the lusts of your father ye will do. He was a murderer from the beginning, and abode not in the truth, because there is no truth in him. When he speaketh a lie, he speaketh of his own: for he is a liar, and the father of it, John 8:44.*

If you are unsaved when Jesus comes and you're left behind to go through the tribulation, you will also be hearing some trumpets, but they will not be the trumpets of God calling believers; they will be the trumpets of judgment as recorded, beginning at *Rev 8:2, And I saw the seven angels which stood before God; and to them were given seven trumpets.* I want you to read with me of these 7 trumpets that are sure to sound in the tribulation of those who are not prepared to meet the Lord in the rapture, and share with you comments from

*Believer's Study Bible. (vv. 7-12) The opening of the
seventh seal initiates the trumpet judgments, just as the
sounding of the seventh trumpet calls for the outpouring
of the bowls of God's wrath. The general significance of
these trumpet judgments may be indicated as follows: The
initial 4 trumpets reveal unprecedented natural calamity
involving immense electrical storms, devastating hail,
volcanic upheaval including pollution of ocean waters, and
cos-mic destruction of stars and other natural lights. The
third trumpet may involve atomic warfare or some other
nuclear catastrophe, which, after taking multitudes of
lives, contaminates the waters and thus brings about the
demise of many more. Listen to **Rev 8:13, And I beheld,
and heard an angel flying through the midst of
heaven, saying with a loud voice, Woe, woe, woe, to the
inhabiters of the earth by reason of the other voices of
the trumpet of the three angels, which are yet to
sound! (9: 3-11)** The nature of these "locusts" is not that
of a physical insect. Their humanlike faces and hair
indicate that they are intelligent spiritual life. They do not
kill, but the torment unleashed on the human family is so
devastating that men seek death, only to find that,
strangely, death flees away. The best interpretation of this
locust plague of the fifth trumpet is that these hideous,
repugnant, and evil creatures are demonic in nature. One
of the ministries of the Holy Spirit in the present
dispensation is the restraining of evil **(2 Thess.
2:6,7)**. This charitable ministry of restraining the
onslaught of evil will be concluded just before the
beginning of the Tribulation, and the end result will be a
devastating invasion of the demonic in the lives of men. So
stringent and devastating is this plague that John
designates it the first of three woes--**Rev 9:12 One woe is***

past; and, behold, there come two woes more hereafter. (vv. 13-19) The sixth trumpet, the second woe, reveals an unprecedented armed assault from across the Euphrates River. Interpreters differ extensively as to the significance of this plague. However, as one seeks to understand the text, it seems appropriate to see the reference to the Euphrates as the literal river. Since spiritual beings are not bound by any river, the more likely understanding is that an actual armed invasion of eastern powers numbering 200,000,000 will plunge the earth into a deadly conflict, resulting in the death of one-third of the earth's population. The description of the horses is such that modern military machines could be intended. Nothing more astonishing could be concluded about the two woes thus far revealed than John's observation that the remainder of the earth's inhabitants are not drawn to repentance by these cataclysmic trumpet judgments. There are two specific categories of unrepentance mentioned: heretical worship (v. 20) and the immorality of men (v. 21). This failure of men to respond appropriately to the judgments of the Tribulation introduces the reader to a crucial aspect of theology. The purpose of the Great Tribulation is to demonstrate the consequences of living under the judgment of God. The goal of such an appeal is to encourage men to repent in light of the certainty of God's eternal retribution, foreshadowed by these tragic years of terrestrial wrath. The result of this last appeal in terms of judgment demonstrates the essential depravity of man. With full cognizance of the judgment of God, men still do not repent.

As I read earlier, the sounding of the seventh trumpet calls for the outpouring of the bowls of God's wrath, recorded beginning in *Rev 16:1 And I heard a great voice out of the temple saying to the seven angels, Go your ways, and pour out the vials of the wrath of God upon the earth.* The vials of wrath—**vv.2-21.**

Those who have *'Christ in you, the hope of glory,' Col 1:27,* will not be here, for we will hear the shout of the Lord, the voice of the arch angel and the trump of God. We and our loved ones who have died 'in Christ' will be with the Lord and *'so shall we ever be with the Lord'.* Listen again to the text of the message--*1 Th 4:16,17.* The Lord can either be your Saviour or judge, which will He be?

This is one of 50 messages from the 'Messages From 1 Thessalonian' series, all of these messages are available on the 'Monitor Messages' CD. It is also one of 89 messages on 'The Time Is At Hand' CD.

Biblical Grounds for Divorce
Matt.5:31,32; 1 Cor.7:10-15

Matthew 5:31-32

31 It hath been said, Whosoever shall put away his wife, let him give her a writing of divorcement:

32 But I say unto you, That whosoever shall put away his wife, saving for the cause of fornication, causeth her to commit adultery: and whosoever shall marry her that is divorced committeth adultery.

1 Corinthians 7:10-15

10 And unto the married I command, *yet* not I, but the Lord, Let not the wife depart from *her* husband:

11 But and if she depart, let her remain unmarried, or be reconciled to *her* husband: and let not the husband put away *his* wife.

12 But to the rest speak I, not the Lord: If any brother hath a wife that believeth not, and she be pleased to dwell with him, let him not put her away.

13 And the woman which hath an husband that believeth not, and if he be pleased to dwell with her, let her not leave him.

¹⁴ For the unbelieving husband is sanctified by the wife, and the unbelieving wife is sanctified by the husband: else were your children unclean; but now are they holy.
¹⁵ But if the unbelieving depart, let him depart. A brother or a sister is not under bondage in such *cases*: but God hath called us to peace.

I preached an earlier message about how the devil deceives the divorced many times to where they feel that have committed a sin which disqualifies them from being effective servants for Christ. I preached another message concerning the marriage relationship; then I preached about what God says about divorce, using the various Scriptures found throughout the Bible. In this message I want you to see what I believe the Bible teaches are grounds for divorce. As with the other messages, perhaps there will be those who will disagree with me who hear the message or read it on the internet. I will deal with the *'except fornication'* clause in our text, as well as the **'not under bondage'** clause in **1 Cor 7:15.**

As I preached earlier, the divine principle for marriage is that it is permanent -*until death do us part.* If it is disrupted, it's contrary to what God intended. Marriage being permanent is a divine principle; the best you can say about divorce is that it is a limited privilege. Our world has departed from divorce being a limited privilege to the point of it being a constitutional right. Really it is a concession to the *'hardness of heart'* so evident in Jesus' day and our own. Jesus answer to those arguing for divorce in *Mat 19 :8, Moses because of the hardness of your hearts suffered you to put away your wives: but from the beginning it was not so.* Too many who are quick to want a divorce, refuse to admit their own *'hardness of heart.'* As a result of this there is escalation of divorce and an erosion of the divine principles of marriage. There is even a worse development: the easing of the procedure for getting a divorce, such as the *'no fault'* divorce. This is an arrangement to terminate a marriage without fixing blame on either party, which saves money and harassment. When a nation's laws starts to tamper with the institution of marriage—especially allowing same-sex marriage, and makes the divorce laws more elastic, it is certain proof of ethical decadence. Having said all this, I want to look at the Scriptural grounds for divorce:

I. The *'except for fornication'* clause--*Mat 19:9, And I say unto you, Whoso-ever shall put away his wife, except it be for fornication, and shall marry another, committeth adultery.* As I stated in a previous message, Jesus did not say *'except it be for adultery'* as many misinterpret this passage. If you use a reference Bible you will find that the cross reference to divorce in *Matt.19:7* and *Matt.5:31* will be to *Deu 24:1, When a man hath taken a wife, and married her, and it come to pass that she find no favour in his eyes, because he hath found some uncleanness in her: then let him write her a bill of divorcement, and give it in her hand, and send her out of his house.* If you will do a study of the phrase *uncleanness in her,* you will find it involved fornication, pre-marital sex as is stated in *Deut. 22:13-15, If any man take a wife, and go in unto her, and hate her, and give occasions of speech against her, and bring up an evil name upon her, and say, I took this woman, and when I came to her, I found her not a maid: then shall the father of the damsel, and her mother, take and bring forth the tokens of the damsel's virginity unto the elders of the city in the gate.* One of the commentaries I read says that the word translated *'fornication', (porneia),* by the time the **Gospel of Matthew** was written, carried the fairly wider meaning of sexual immorality. As stated in a previous message, it means unmarried sexual relationships, and may also include homosexuality, lesbianism, improper sexual desires and demands, incest, sadomasochism, bestiality, pornography, or other sexual perversions.

What about the sin of adultery, unfaithfulness in marriage? It was punishable by death, as I noted previously; this would free the innocent to remarry for it says in **1 Cor 7:39, The wife is bound by the law as long as her husband liveth; but if her husband be dead, she is at liberty to be married to whom she will; only in the Lord.** Some commentaries rightly state that the fornication referred to in **Deu 24:1,** is not equivalent with adultery, under the law, as adultery was punishable by death. Their argument is the **Gospel of Mattthew** was primarily written to the Jews, and the other Gospel's cross-references to this passage in **Mark** and **Luke,** which were written to the Gentiles, where the **'except'** clause is not found—**Mark 10:11 And he saith unto them, Whosoever shall put away his wife, and marry another, committeth adultery against her. Lk. 16:18, Whosoever putteth away his wife, and marrieth another, committeth adultery: and whosoever** *marrieth her that is put away from her husband committeth adultery.* They say the *'except it be for fornication'* clause therefore applies to Israel and the Law of Moses and to use these verses from *Matthew* as grounds for divorce is opposed to other Biblical passages which teach that we are to follow the example in *Eph 4:31, 32, Let all bitterness, and wrath, and anger, and clamour, and evil speaking, be put away from you, with all malice: and be ye kind one to another, tenderhearted, forgiving one another, even as God for Christ's sake hath forgiven you.* This is a text I use a lot in counseling.

I've seen marriages saved, even after infidelity, by those who were forgiven and were forgiving. As stated in a previous message, *'When a separation or divorce occurs, always seek reconciliation as long as the possibility exists.'* Divorce not only hurts the two subjects involved, but affects others as well, especially if there are children involved. Just because one may feel they have grounds for divorce does not mean that it is best for them to go ahead and carry it through. If God in His mercy has forgiven you of your sins, then should you not forgive the guilty one, in order to save the marriage and not break up the home? *Mat 6:14,15, For if ye forgive men their trespasses, your heavenly Father will also forgive you: but if ye forgive not men their trespasses, neither will your Father forgive your trespasses.*

My point is this, I believe that it is my duty as a pastor and counselor to try to preserve as many marriages as I can. However, there are situations where there are irreconcilable differences, where usually the guilty party will not give up their sinful lifestyle of fornication, whether it be unfaithfulness, or one of the many other sins that comes under the broader spectrum of the sin of fornication, as previously stated. Jesus said that fornication was grounds for divorce—*Mat 19:9, And I say unto you, Whosoever shall put away his wife, except it be for fornication, and shall marry another, committeth adultery.* The practice of easy divorce that many of the Jews were practicing in Jesus time was based on—*It hath been said.* What was being said, *Whosoever shall put away his wife, let him give her a writing of divorcement, Mat 5:31.* Was the Samaritan woman a victim of easy divorce? *(John 4:18) H*ere is what He said in *Mat 5:32, But I say unto you, That whosoever shall put away his wife, saving for the cause of fornication, causeth her to commit adultery: and whosoever shall marry her that is divorced committeth adultery.* The passage in *Mat 19:9* concerns the man marrying another committing adultery, and here it is the woman remarrying committing adultery. Divorce on unbiblical grounds complicates sin rather than cures it, and may implicate others in sin rather than absolve them.

So we come to the question, *Are there Biblical grounds for divorce where one or the other commits fornication?* Yes, I believe there may be grounds for divorce, but I will do all within my power, as I trust the Lord for giving the right Scriptural counsel, to save the marriage. Then we find the . . .

II. *'Not under bondage'* clause in *1 Cor 7:15.* Vincent *Word Studies* says of this verse and the word *'bondage'*—*'A strong word, indicating Christianity has not made marriage a state of slavery to believers. The meaning clearly is that willful desertion on the part of the unbelieving husband or wife sets the other party free. Such cases are not comprehended in Christ's words.'* **'God hath called us to peace'**--Vincent writes, *'Enslavement in the marriage relation between the believer and unbeliever is contrary to the spirit and intent of this calling.'* Listen to the context of this verse *(vv.10-15).* Some may say, *'But this is Paul speaking, not the Lord' (v.12).* We must under-stand Paul wrote by apostolic authority, and under the inspiration of the Holy Spirit. He's saying, *'The Lord dealt with the subject of divorce and remarriage as related to fornication and unfaithfulness, but I write to you who are living in an 'unequal yoke.'* He meant that there was no direct command given by the Lord Jesus on the subject of believers and unbelievers being married. Paul writes, **Be ye not unequally yoked together with unbelievers in 2 Cor.6:14.** It is wrong for believers to marry unbelievers, but the situation that existed in Corinth was that some were being saved and their marriage partner was still in a heathen religion and was giving them much opposition.

A. The believer was to continue living with the unsaved *(vv.12,13).* They were not to initiate separation.

B. The reason given is that the unsaved has a greater chance of being saved by the sanctifying presence of the believer in the home *(14a: 1 Pet.3:1,2,7)* The children also will learn by the believer's perseverance and faith in undesirable circumstances *(14b).*

C. A very common thing in the first century, because the marriage contract was easily broken, was that heathen husbands frequently left their wives and heathen wives deserted their husbands over the matter of their new found faith in Jesus Christ. Where did this leave the believer? *A brother or sister is not under bondage in such cases, v.15.* A common thing in our own time is that many times in a Christian marriage one will depart from the faith, fall into sin, and choose to leave the one they are married to. The question is, can we apply this Scripture *in such cases?* I believe we can. True, Christ did not speak to this issue, but again we need to recognize Paul wrote under the inspiration of the Holy Spirit concerning a situation which existed in his day and in a real sense can be applied to the situation in our present day where many fall into sin and leave their spouse.

What does *'not under bondage'* mean? Is Paul contradicting himself if we interpret this passage as saying one can be freed from the marriage contract in such cases, when we compare it with *v.39.* The word **'bound'** is translated from the Greek word 'deo', which means 'to bind, be in bonds'. Paul is saying according to the law, marriage is a life-long monogamous union. In dealing with law and sin, Paul reiterates what God's original plan in marriage should be in *Rom.7:1-3.* The word *'bondage' (v.15)* is translated from the Greek word *'douloo'* (douluw), which means *'to bring into (under) bondage.'* I believe it says that if the unbeliever departs and is unwilling to continue the marriage, *'in such cases'* 'the believer is to let them go, and they may be divorced, freed from the marriage contract and may remarry. But please note, it is the unbeliever that departs, not the believer, and I believe the unbeliever (the guilty party) would commit adultery if they remarry or have a relationship with the opposite sex.

III. Since I believe there are Scriptural grounds for divorce, then what is the Scriptural method to obtain a divorce, if the guilty party has been forgiven of their sin, and the innocent party is a believer. In other words, if both are now forgiven believers in Christ. If we use the Bible for grounds for divorce, then we should use the Bible in obtaining a divorce. No doubt this will be something you have never heard in divorce proceedings, but I feel if this method prescribed by the Bible was followed we would see many   broken relationships restored and marriages saved.

A. The first principle is that we as believers are not to go before sinners with matters pertaining to personal offences *(1 Cor.6:1-7)*. This also teaches, that for the sake of Christian testimony, we may suffer fraud *(v.7)*.

B. How are we to handle personal problems *(Matt.18:15-17)*. 1) The first step is to seek reconciliation *(Matt.18:15)*. 2) Then take one or two witnesses and continue seeking reconciliation *(v.16)*. Witnesses establish every word. 3) If they still refuse counsel, it should be brought before the whole church, then if they still neglect reconciliation, *'let him (her) be as a heathen and a publican' (v.17)*. *'But if the unbelieving depart, let him depart. A brother or a sister is not under bondage in such cases.' (1 Cor.7:*

15).

IV. Since I believe there are Scriptural grounds for divorce, does this mean that one is free to marry? After the woman is divorced what does it say in **Deut.24:2?** Do they commit adultery if they marry someone who has not been married before, or one who is a widow or widower, or one who has been freed from a previous marriage partner on Scriptural grounds?

A. The answer is found in *1 Cor.7:27,28.*

B. If a couple insisted on marriage, they would not sin, but they may be asking for problems, which he wanted to spare them *(v.28b).*

In this series of messages I have shared with you some things I believe the Bible says about divorce and remarriage. As I said in the opening message, there are different opinions held on the subject of divorce and consequently there is much confusion about what the Bible says. You may have agreed with all I have said, or with very little I have said, but I have endeavored to let the Word of God speak the truth objectively to us. It would have been easier to lightly pass over this part of the Sermon on the Mount and not deal with it, as many are doing in our day, for fear of offending someone who holds a different view. However, I feel it is an issue which needs to be dealt with and I have sensed the Holy Spirit's guidance as I accepted the challenge and prepared the messages.

In the beginning I preached on how *'the devil deceives the divorced'* as they are plagued with guilt feelings and let the devil bring defeat in their life, rather than seeking a new and vital relationship with the Lord. I preached a message concerning the marriage relationship being God-ordained from the beginning and that God intended it to be a life-long, monogamous union; that it is a binding covenant, and should be entered into cautiously, prayerfully, and Scripturally (in the Lord). Then I preached a message on what God says about divorce (putting away) in the Word, considering each passage in its context. I did emphasize **Mal.2:16,** where it says that God, *'hateth putting away.'* I preached a message on the *'Ten Commandments of Marriage,'* which is a preventive message from there being marriage problems that may lead to divorce. Then this final messages on 'Biblical Grounds For Divorce'. I believe I have been thorough in my study for all of these messages and I myself came to some conclusions that I did not previously have on what the Bible teaches concerning divorce.

This is one of 5 messages on marriage, divorce, and remarriage from the 'Sermon on the Mount' series, of which there are a total of 55 messages. All these messages are available on the 'Monitor Messages' CD

Seeking God is Essential
Heb.11:6

But without faith it is impossible to please him: for he that cometh to God must believe that he is, and that he is a rewarder of them that diligently seek him.

You may wonder why I am preaching from **v.6** when I haven't preached on **v.5** concerning Enoch walking with God. I have already preached several messages on faith and one of the messages was *'We Can Be Heroes'.* I believe **v.6** sums up what needs to be said about faith before we look at Enoch and the others listed as *'heroes of faith.'* If we as God's people ever accomplish anything for Him it will be by having our faith in Him.

I am preaching on *'Seeking God is Essential.'* True faith is the most active force in the world, it will affect one's life like nothing else. Important truths found in the Bible, if really believed, will touch every nerve of one's body

and cause one to conform to what it says in *Rom 12:1,2* .
. by the mercies of God, that ye present your bodies a
living sacrifice, holy, acceptable unto God, which is
your reasonable service. And be not conformed to this
world: but be ye transformed by the renewing of your
mind, that ye may prove what is that good, and
acceptable, and perfect, will of God.

Without faith you are without God; without faith you
are without hope; and sinners without faith you are
without a Savior! When I say faith, what am I talking
about? In our Evangelism Explosion training we see
kinds of faith mentioned which are not saving and
trusting faith. There is the *historical faith* that one may
give mental assent to. One may believe that the Bible is
the inspired Word of God but not accept its truth in their
heart. One can believe all the Bible says about Jesus--that
He was virgin born, lived a perfect sinless life, died on the
cross for the sins of the world, that He was buried, rose
again the third day, that He ascended back to the right
hand of the Father to intercede for sinners and that He's
coming again. Mental assent to the truths of the Bible is
a mere passive faith that is believed but not acted
upon. The devil and his demons have such a belief-
James 2:19, Thou believest that there is one God; thou
doest well: the devils also believe, and tremble.

Then there is a *temporal faith*--people pray when they
have problems--child is sick, finances are low, business
is bad. This is a little deeper than the intellectual assent
that there is a God, as they actually seem to trust Him for
some things. Many unsaved people whisper a prayer
when they board an airplane. But this is not the kind of

faith our text is about--calling on God when you need Him as the hypocrite in *Job 27:8-10, For what is the hope of the hypocrite, though he hath gained, when God taketh away his soul? Will God hear his cry when trouble cometh upon him? Will he delight himself in the Almighty? Will he always call upon God?*

Many have a *'trust in works'* faith for salvation—*'I try to live a good life; I live by the Golden Rule.'* They have an *'I'* problem--I do this--I do that. *Eph 2:8,9, For by grace are ye saved through faith; and that not of yourselves: it is the gift of God: not of works, lest any man should boast.* Then I've seen some who have a *temporary faith* when you witness to them, it seems they are saved—*Lk. 8:13 'when they hear, receive the word with joy; and these have no root, which for a while believe, and in time of temptation fall away.'*

There are three key words in the text which helps us to understand what it is saying in-*Heb 11:6, But without faith it is <u>impossible</u> to please him: for he that cometh to God <u>must</u> believe that he is, and that he is a rewarder of them that <u>diligently</u> seek him.* The first key word I want to look at is:

I. Impossible. The necessity of faith is strongly asserted! This applies to both the saved and unsaved. If sinners are ever saved, they will be saved the way God says *for by grace are ye saved through faith.* If you have been saved it is evident throughout the Bible that you cannot, *it is impossible,* please God unless you continue to walk in faith. A continuous faith is taught clearly in this verse--*he that cometh to God. 'Cometh' is* a continuous verb and does not just apply when you first come to Him for salvation.

This law of impossibility is universal to every form of work or worship. It doesn't make any difference what we do, without faith in God it is impossible to please Him. Sinners will never get to heaven on their good merits; those of you who have trusted in Christ for salvation need to understand that without faith your desires and efforts won't amount to a plug nickel-i.e., worship and sacrifice without faith, as we saw with Cain; witnessing without faith; praying without faith is useless.

It doesn't say, without faith it is difficult to please God--it is **impossible!** Do you have the kind of faith that leads to action? Right after it says **the devils also believe, and tremble---James 2:20, But wilt thou know, O vain man, that faith without works is dead?** Are there some that you want to see saved? Do you have faith that they will be saved? What have you done about having your prayers answered for their salvation? If you have done what you can, then you need to believe [have faith] they will be saved. The story is told of a college student who had answered the call to preach. He had preached earnestly several times, but he was concerned that he had not seen any conversions. He came to an older preacher with his concern and the older preacher asked him, *'Do you believe that every time you preach the Word that hearts will be touched and lives changed?'* The young preacher replied, *'No, I don't expect that!'* The old preacher replied, *'That is why God is not blessing your ministry, because you have no faith in Him.'* **(Heb.11:1)**

II. 'Must' is the next word in our text I want to emphasize. *Heb 11:6, But without faith it is impossible to please him: for he that cometh to God must believe that he is, and that he is a rewarder of them that diligently seek him.* It doesn't say *"should"* but it says *"must,"* a much stronger word--**must believe that he is.**

A. There is a God that exists. He is not some abstract force or power, as the philosophies of the world and the liberals teach. One must accept God as He is revealed in Scripture. He is a personal being, Who is a sovereign God that can act in behalf of your needs, as well as our sinful deeds.

B. He is a holy God. We *must believe that he is,* we *must not* try to fashion a *'god'* such as we would like to have, that would be idolatry. We must see Him as Isaiah saw Him *(Isa.6:1-5).* Holiness is not relative! That's what's wrong with the church today! No wonder we are not reaching the world for Christ! A lot of it is because of the preachers who will preach against sin as long as it doesn't offend anyone in their congregation. They will preach against tobacco as long as they are not in NC. They will preach against indecent dress as long as they are not preaching in Virginia Beach or Florida. Some lily-livered preachers will move to an area where something is going on in church, or in the area, and something they preached against at the church they just moved from, then they won't speak out against that same sin. They are afraid to call sin *'sin.'* You know why? They are afraid they will lose their job. You know what the Bible calls what they are paid for their inoffensive preaching? *'Filthy lucre.'* That term is used 5 times in N.T. and refers to the preacher with the exception of one time where it is used of the deacon in *1 Tim 3:8.* Listen to *Tit.1:9-13.* The whole point of what I've said is this: You must see God as He is--a holy God. It my duty as your preacher to preach His holiness and if you are living in sin you need that kind of preaching to convict you of sin and bring you to repentance. I am not ashamed to be called a *'holiness preacher'!*

   C. The verse not only implies that there is a God, that He's a holy God, but it also says that you must believe in His presence—*'He is.'* He is where I am. God is everywhere, therefore, I dare not offend His holiness any place. Believer, this will make your prayer life effective, if you have had trouble praying as you should- *Isa 59:1,2, Behold, the Lord's hand is not shortened, that it cannot save; neither his ear heavy, that it cannot hear: But your iniquities have separated between you and your God, and your sins have hid his face from you, that he will not hear.* Always remember that *'He is'*—He is there where you work; in your recreation time; in your living room as you sit and watch 'slop operas' and the perverts which entertain on TV and videos. Do you believe that *'He is' t*hat He is there? If there is a place on earth where God is not, you could go there and sin, not offending His holiness--but there is no such spot in the whole universe-*Psa 139:7 Whither shall I go from thy spirit? or whither shall I flee from thy presence?* *'He is'*--He knows what you do, He is aware of all we say, He even knows what you are thinking-*Psa 139:2, Thou understandest my thought* *afar off.* That being the case, we need to pray as the Psalmist-*Psa 139:23,24 Search me, O God, and know my heart: try me, and know my thoughts: And see if there be any wicked way in me, and lead me in the way everlasting.* Remember our text says, *He that cometh to God must believe that he is.*

III. The third and final word I want you to see in our text is *'diligently.'*

What does *'diligently'* mean? Strong's--*to search out, investigate, crave, demand, worship, inquire (require), seek after (carefully, diligently).* What I have said is, if you don't have the right kind of faith it is impossible to please Him, consequently you will not be seeking Him as you must. If you don't believe that *'He is'*-that He is a real personal God, a sovereign God, a Holy God, and One that is everywhere present, then you are not diligently seeking Him. To diligently seek is a very strong expression in the Greek. *Illus. of diligence-If your child was lost you would call everyone you know to help find your child. You wouldn't half-heartedly seek, you would spend all the time necessary. You would want every available resource put at your disposal--helicopters, blood hounds, etc.*

Believers if we want to be rewarded with revival in the church and seeing lost people saved, then we must do as our text says-*He is a rewarder of them that diligently seek him.* If we want revival we will have the kind of faith that pleases Him; we will believe that *He is*-that He knows all about our need for revival, we will be diligently seeking Him in prayer, not only for our need of revival, but also for the spiritual needs of those who are on our prayer list. If we follow the teaching of our text verse, then we can claim the promise of *James 5:16, The effectual fervent prayer of a righteous man availeth much.*

I want to close with this thought in mind. We are now an organized church, and that means we no longer depend upon the mission board or others to help us. It means we ought to **diligently** do all we can to see our church grow in number and in spirit. But as I said in this morning's message, there will be no *'reaping in joy'* or *'rejoicing' u*ntil there is some *'sowing in tears a*nd bearing precious seed.'* I*f there is to be revival, if we are rewarded with souls being saved, we must seek revival- ***But without faith it is impossible to please him: for he that cometh to God must believe that he is, and that he is a rewarder of them that diligently seek him Heb 11:6.*** If we want our prayers answered in the lives of those we are praying for, then we must in faith, believe that God will speak to their hearts as we witness to them, that He will convict them of their sin, and that they will come in repentance and belief in Jesus Christ's life blood to cover their sins, as He died for our sins.

To any unsaved, or living in unbelief, I want to give you the opportunity to come to the Rewarder in our text. *Who is it that you must come to?* **To God.** *How are you to come?* You must come in faith believing that He will cleanse you of all sin in your life-***If we confess our sins, he is faithful and just to forgive us our sins, and to cleanse us from all unrighteousness, 1 John 1:9***

This is the ninth of 41 messages preached in the series, 'Living By Faith' series from Hebrews 11, available on the 'Monitor Messages' CD

Acts of the Apostates
Jude 1-25

¹ Jude, the servant of Jesus Christ, and brother of James, to them that are sanctified by God the Father, and preserved in Jesus Christ, and called:

² Mercy unto you, and peace, and love, be multiplied.

³ Beloved, when I gave all diligence to write unto you of the common salvation, it was needful for me to write unto you, and exhort you that ye should earnestly contend for the faith which was once delivered unto the saints.

⁴ For there are certain men crept in unawares, who were before of old ordained to this condemnation, ungodly men, turning the grace of our God into lasciviousness, and denying the only Lord God, and our Lord Jesus Christ.

⁵ I will therefore put you in remembrance, though ye once knew this, how that the Lord, having saved the people out of the land of Egypt, afterward destroyed them that believed not.

⁶ And the angels which kept not their first estate, but left their own habitation, he hath reserved in everlasting chains under darkness unto the judgment of the great day.

7 Even as Sodom and Gomorrha, and the cities about them in like manner, giving themselves over to fornication, and going after strange flesh, are set forth for an example, suffering the vengeance of eternal fire.

8 Likewise also these filthy dreamers defile the flesh, despise dominion, and speak evil of dignities.

9 Yet Michael the archangel, when contending with the devil he disputed about the body of Moses, durst not bring against him a railing accusation, but said, The Lord rebuke thee.

10 But these speak evil of those things which they know not: but what they know naturally, as brute beasts, in those things they corrupt themselves.

11 Woe unto them! for they have gone in the way of Cain, and ran greedily after the error of Balaam for reward, and perished in the gainsaying of Core.

12 These are spots in your feasts of charity, when they feast with you, feeding themselves without fear: clouds they are without water, carried about of winds; trees whose fruit withereth, without fruit, twice dead, plucked up by the roots;

13 Raging waves of the sea, foaming out their own shame; wandering stars, to whom is reserved the blackness of darkness for ever.

14 And Enoch also, the seventh from Adam, prophesied of these, saying, Behold, the Lord cometh with ten thousands of his saints,

15 To execute judgment upon all, and to convince all that are ungodly among them of all their ungodly deeds which they have ungodly committed, and of all their hard speeches which ungodly sinners have spoken against him.

16 These are murmurers, complainers, walking after their

own lusts; and their mouth speaketh great swelling words, having men's persons in admiration because of advantage.
17 But, beloved, remember ye the words which were spoken before of the apostles of our Lord Jesus Christ;
18 How that they told you there should be mockers in the last time, who should walk after their own ungodly lusts.
19 These be they who separate themselves, sensual, having not the Spirit.
20 But ye, beloved, building up yourselves on your most holy faith, praying in the Holy Ghost,
21 Keep yourselves in the love of God, looking for the mercy of our Lord Jesus Christ unto eternal life.
22 And of some have compassion, making a difference:
23 And others save with fear, pulling them out of the fire; hating even the garment spotted by the flesh.
24 Now unto him that is able to keep you from falling, and to present you faultless before the presence of his glory with exceeding joy,
25 To the only wise God our Saviour, be glory and majesty, dominion and power, both now and ever. Amen.

I've read to you the entire book of Jude, one of the most neglected books in the Bible. I have never preached through this short book. As I read it over again this week, I have come to believe that in these last days we are living in, it is a book that needs to read and preached, as it warns us of encountering the apostates. S. Maxwell Coder says in his commentary on Jude: The beginning of the church is described in the **Acts of the Apostles.** The end of the Church Age is set forth in the Epistle of Jude, which might well be called the *'Acts of the Apostates'.* The first epistle after the Gospels, Acts, can properly be said to contain Church history describing the deeds and teachings of men of God through whom Christ began to build His Church. The last epistle, Jude, before the Book of Revelation relates the deeds and teaching of evil men who will be living upon the earth as the history of the professing Church comes to an end.

Jude is the only book in all God's Word entirely devoted to the great apostasy which is to come upon Christendom before the Lord Jesus Christ returns. This brief book of twenty-five verses is the doorway to the Revelation, giving us the apocalyptic judgments unfolded therein.

Without Jude, the prophetic picture which begins with the teachings of Christ in the Gospels and develops throughout the epistles would be incomplete. Paul supplied us with the terminology commonly used by Bible students concerning a falling away from the faith of our fathers in the last days. He called it *'apostasy'. **2 Th 2:3, Let no man deceive you by any means: for that day shall not come, except there come a falling away first, and that man of sin be revealed, the son of perdition.** The **falling away** is a translation of the Geek word *'apostasia'*, from which we get the word *'apostasy.'* You will find in Strong's that it means; *defection from truth; apostasy--falling away, forsake.* He described it as a departure from the faith in **1 Tim 4:1, Now the Spirit speaketh expressly, that in the latter times some shall depart from the faith, giving heed to seducing spirits, and doctrines of devils;** he tells us it is an unwillingness to endure sound doctrine, **For the time will come when** *they will not endure sound doctrine; but after their own lusts shall they heap to themselves teachers, having itching ears.* Through the apostle Peter, the Holy Spirit revealed that false teachers would someday appear and bring in *'damnable heresies, even denying the Lord that bought them,' 2 Pet 2:1.*

The possibility that the denial of faith, so widespread in our own generation, may be a prelude to the great apostasy referred to by Jesus in *Lk.18:8, When the Son of man cometh, shall he find faith on the earth? T*his should quicken our interest in this final epistle during these momentous times. If the last page of history of the Church about to be turned, we may expect the Holy Spirit to give us new light on the strange and terrible words and warnings of Jude. A fresh study may awaken us to a solemn realization that it is later than we think, so that we shall pray and work as never before, for an ingathering of many souls before the great and terrible day of the Lord shall come.

I will be preaching a series on *'The Acts of the Apostates,'* and this first message will be from *vv.1,2.* These verses tell us who the letter is from, who it is to, and what the writer wants for his readers.

I. The letter is from Jude. As Paul, in the first word of his epistles, he identifies that it is from *Jude.* In the original Greek, this name is Judas. In the very first word of a book about apostasy appears a name which brings to mind a traitor who stands forever as the worst apostate the world has ever known—Judas who betrayed our Lord for 30 pieces of silver. Judas was a common name at that time, but is not common today, as you will not find one named Judas today. But God chose *Jude* [Judas], *the servant of Jesus Christ'*, to inspire and write this short letter on apostasy that we will be looking at in the coming weeks.

You will note that he gives his heavenly relationship before he gave his earthly relationship--*the servant of Jesus Christ.* He was among the few *servants of Jesus Christ* who were chosen to write under the inspiration of God the Bible we have today. *Knowing this first that no prophecy of the scripture is of any private interpretation. For the prophecy came not in old time by the will of man: but holy men of God spake as they were moved by the Holy Ghost, 2 Pet 1:20 21.* When he says that he is a *servant of Jesus Christ,* literally means that he was Christ's bondslave. As he put our blessed Lord first, we too should have Him as the absolute Lord of our lives.

Next he gives his earthly relationship. There are differences of opinion which Jude is the writer of the letter. I personally believe, as it says, that he Jude, was a *'brother of James,'* who was head of the church at Jerusalem, and author of the Epistle of James. James is called *'the Lord's brother' (Gal.1:19).* This means that Jude was one of the four brothers of the Lord Jesus mentioned in *Mark 6:3,* who grew up with Him in Nazareth. There were those in the synagogue who doubted His deity, that He was the God-man Jesus Christ and they asked,*Is not this the carpenter, the son of Mary, the brother of James, and Joses, and of Juda, and Simon? And are not his sisters here with us? Mark*

6:3. *T*here is the prophecy in *Psa.69:7,8* *e*ven Christ's own family wouldn't believe Him for who He was: *Because for thy sake I have borne reproach; shame hath covered my face. I am become a stranger unto my brethren, and an alien unto my mother's children.* That prophecy was fulfilled in *John 7:5, For neither did his brethren believe in him.* With humility or perhaps because they did not believe on Him at one time, neither of the brothers mentions his human relationship to the Lord Jesus. One writer says, Great honor would be attached to that relationship, and it is possible that the reason why it was not referred to by James and Jude was an apprehension that it might produce jealousy, as if they claimed some special pre-eminence over their brethren. The books these brothers wrote present one similarity in content. James sets forth good works as real evidence of saving faith; Jude sets forth evil works as real evidence of apostasy.

II. Who is the epistle of Jude to? *Verse 1* is commonly called in a letter the salutation. It is to us today and to all *'that are sanctified by God the Father, and preserved in Jesus Christ, and called.'* Mathew Henry notes: *Jude is addressed to all believers in the gospel. Its design appears to be to guard believers against the false teachers who had begun to creep into the Christian church, and to scatter dangerous tenets, by attempting to lower all Christianity into a merely nominal belief and outward profession of the gospel.* Note the Trinity is involved in our salvation. Our calling is the work of the *Holy Spirit;* we are sanctified by the *Father;* we are kept in *Jesus Christ.* This threefold declaration presents a most astonishing and comforting series of truths for the encouragement of all God's people in days of darkness, delusion and doctrines of demons within the professing Church. God assures our hearts that He has called us, that He loves us, and that He is keeping us for His Son, no matter what happens around us. Although we are kept *[preserved]*, according to *v.1,* we are nevertheless to *keep ourselves in the love of God. vv.20,21, But ye, beloved, building up yourselves on your most holy faith, praying in the Holy Ghost, keep yourselves in the love of God, looking for the mercy of our Lord Jesus Christ unto eternal life.* And His part and promise is given in *v.24, Now unto him that is able to keep you from falling, and to present you faultless before the presence of his glory with exceeding joy.* Again we see there is God's side to the blessed truth of perseverance, as well as our side. This stated in our Free Will Baptist Treatise: *'There are strong grounds to hope that the truly regenerate will persevere unto the end, and be saved, through the power of divine grace which is pledged to their support.'*

Jude is to the sanctified, those who are set apart at salvation and are continuing to *'cleanse themselves from all filthiness of the flesh and spirit, perfecting holiness in the fear of God,' 2 Cor 7:1.* Jude is to *them that are sanctified by God the Father, and preserved in Jesus Christ, and called.* Who are the called? The Scriptures reply: *God hath from the beginning chosen you to salvation through sanctification of the Spirit and belief of the truth: whereunto he called you by our gospel, to the obtaining of the glory of our Lord Jesus Christ. 2 Ths 2:13,14.* This is not teaching predestination. Those who are called are those who, hearing the Gospel, have been so deeply convicted by the Holy Spirit that they have believed the truth and received the Saviour who died for their sins and rose again from the dead. They have been brought *'out of darkness into his marvelous light' (1 Peter 2:9).* The Saviour issued the call, *'Come unto me.'* Jude addresses his epistle to all who have heard this call and responded. He calls those *'beloved'* who he is addressing the letter to in *v.3.* Who are the *'beloved'?* The Lord Jesus said in *John 16:27, For the Father himself loveth you, because ye have loved me, and have believed that I came out from God.*

III. What Jude wants for his readers is *'mercy unto you, and peace and love, be multiplied.* This epistle has to do with apostasy in the last time--*How that they told you there should be mockers in the last time, who should walk after their own ungodly lusts, v.18.* God's people will need mercy in these days. Mercy is divine pity expressing itself in help for the needy. It presupposes need and helplessness.

A. *Mercy* stands over the threshold of this epistle of the apostasy, introducing a somber picture. I think everyone would agree we are living in a day of apostasy, as we see where whole denominations that were once were true to the Word of God departing from the faith. *Eph.2* speaks of the grace of God to us who *'in time past ye walked according to the course of this world, according to the prince of the power of the air, the spirit that now worketh in the children of disobedience, v.2.* And how *'by grace are ye saved through faith' v.8.* and *'that in the ages to come he might show the exceeding riches of his grace in his* *kindness toward us through Christ Jesus,' v.7.* Grace opens upon the riches of undeserved favor. But God is also rich in mercy—*'God, who is rich in mercy, for his great love wherewith he loved us, v.4.* He exhorts us in His Word to *'come boldly to the throne of grace, that we may obtain mercy, and find grace to help in time of need,' Heb. 4:16.* Jude assures us that such a time will surely come, and we can see the days of apostasy are now here.

B. *Peace* is the second great Bible word to be multiplied for believers in these last days. There is no peace for the wicked *(Isa. 57:20, 21),* but as believers persevere *'we have peace with God through our Lord Jesus Christ,' Rom. 5:1.* In these last days when many are turning from faith we will need more of the peace of God, which passeth all understanding. *Phil 4:6,7, Be careful for nothing; but in everything by prayer and supplication with thanksgiving let your requests be made known unto God. And the peace of God, which passeth all understanding, shall keep your hearts and minds through Christ Jesus.* D. L. Moody wrote in the margin of his Bible at these verses concerning the peace we have: *'This is ours when we worry about nothing, pray about everything, thank God for anything.'* Peace is the stronghold of our hearts until the Lord comes and takes us to our eternal peace.

C. The third word we find is *love,* the bond uniting believers to their Lord and to one another. It is the first commandment of Christ: *'A new commandment I give unto you, that ye love one another. ... By this shall all men know that ye are my disciples,' John 13:34,35.* We need one another in these last days of apostasy.

We have the mercy of God, the peace of God, the love of God. They reappear at the close of the epistle, bringing into focus the holy Trinity once more. We are to **keep ourselves in the love of God, , looking for the mercy of our Lord Jesus Christ unto eternal life v. 21,** to keep **'praying in the Holy Ghost,' v. 20,** which is the key to the experience of the peace of God in **Phil. 4:6, 7.**

There is an upward look in the word **mercy,** an inward look in the word **peace,** an outward look in the word **love.** These three relate us properly to God, to our own inner being, to our brethren around us. When they are multiplied, and only then, will we be able to cope with the great apostasy of the last days.

This is the first of 20 messages preached from the short Book of Jude in the 'Acts of the Apostates' series available on the 'Monitor Messages' CD.

What is Wrong With . . . ?
Heb.12:1,2

1 Wherefore seeing we also are compassed about with so great a cloud of witnesses, let us lay aside every weight, and the sin which doth so easily beset us, and let us run with patience the race that is set before us,
2 Looking unto Jesus the author and finisher of our faith; who for the joy that was set before him endured the cross, despising the shame, and is set down at the right hand of the throne of God.

Bro. Christian Powell (NC) preached a great message on the besetting sins that we as believers may have in our lives at the Preaching Conference in Pigeon Forge. He used as an illustration *'Achilles' heel'*, pointing out that it was a myth of the Greeks. The story is when Achilles was born, his mother tried to make him immortal by dipping him in the river Styx. According to Greek mythology as she immersed him, she held him by one heel and forgot to dip him a second time so the heel she held could get wet too. Therefore, the place where she held him remained untouched by the magic water of the Styx River and that part stayed mortal or vulnerable. Years later as a grown man and warrior he had killed one of his enemy's brothers and this enemy called upon the Greek god Apollo in seeking revenge on Achilles. As his enemy shot an arrow at random, do you know the place on his body where he was mortally wounded? His heel! To this day, any weak point is called an *'Achilles' heel'*. The encyclopedia says, relative to its use, *an Achilles' heel is a fatal weakness in spite of overall strength, actually or potentially leading to downfall.*

In believer's lives there are weaknesses that are their *'Achilles' heel'* that may lead to their downfall. In the text they are **'every weight, and the sin which doth so easily beset us.'** I preached a message a couple years ago from this text, *Running the Race to Win.'* We are in a race and we are nearing the finish line, and it had better be in our hearts to win. In the days when Paul wrote his epistles, the Greeks paid a lot of attention to physical culture, the development of muscles, the proportion of the limbs to one another, the production of everything in the body which might conduce to the soundness of manhood. Paul wrote to Timothy in **1 Tim 4:7,8 ..Exercise thyself rather unto godliness. For bodily exercise profiteth little: but godliness is profitable unto all things, having promise of the life that now is, and of that which is to come.** The word **'exercise'** comes from the same Greek word from which we get the word *'gymnasium',* so we see here that Paul is using an illustration of physical fitness to teach the importance of spiritual fitness. Our text is obviously referring to a foot race, and physically speaking a runner must take away any weights that would hinder him winning the race. I do want to say that it is not a 100 yard dash that we are in as believers, but it is more like a marathon. I found it interesting that the word *'beset'* literally means *'standing around'*. In other words, instead of being in the race we are standing around on the sidelines. I don't want that to be true of any believer here today. Though *'Achilles' heel'* is a myth, I want you to understand that **'weights and besetting sins'** are not a myth, but a fact!

Before I get into the message I want to say there are some things that may be **'weights'** that are not necessarily sins, but when one allows them to hinder his Christian race, they may cause you to lose the race. When **'weights'** or things hinder your devotion time, your prayer time, your attendance at church, your failing to witness and visit lost people, those weights become sins. ***James 4:17, To him that knoweth to do good and doeth it not, to him it is sin***

Did you notice the title of this message in the bulletin? *'What is Wrong With . . . ?'* and you can put in there some of the **'weights and besetting sins'** that many don't deal with in their lives and are living defeated Christian lives, or they are backslidden away from God. When anyone comes to me and asked me, *'What is wrong with [whatever it is],* I know that the Lord is dealing with them about it. Many times I will tell them when in doubt, don't do it.

I am going to do something I have never done, as I want your input into some messages and fact sheets about anything you may have questions about. I have talked with Bro. John about this and he will be assisting me in getting the facts about some sins and weights that will hinder, or may be hindering some of you in your Christian race. I know he has heard from the young people, as I have from adults—'what is wrong with..' We will deal some of these *'weights and besetting sins'* in a series of topical messages and fact sheets on some sins that will be presented in such a way so as not to judge, but to bring conviction of sin in people's lives. How can we accomplish this and see your victory over your 'Achilles' heel'—the weaknesses you may have in your life? We will do so by answering the question *'What is wrong with [whatever it is]?* with the *following questions: What does the Bible say about it? How does it hinder my relationship with God? How will it affect, not only my testimony, but the image of Christ and our church to others? Am I willing to repent of it and seek God's power, rather than my own power to overcome it?*

I. What does the Bible say about it? This is the most important question to be asked about anything? As I said in a previous message, many people say they believe in a literal interpretation of Scripture until it literally speaks about some besetting sin in their lives. It is always easier for us to see sin in other's lives and judge them. Jesus spoke of this in the Sermon on the Mount. *Mat 7:3, And why beholdest thou the mote* [a splinter] *that is in thy brother's eye, but considerest not the beam* [log] *that is in thine own eye? S*o as we deal with the besetting sins, don't be guilty of being blind to your own weaknesses. If you think you can live above sin, listen to what those of us read this week who are reading the Bible through--*Prov 20:9, Who can say, I have made my heart clean, I am pure from my sin?* It says in *1 John 1:8, If we say that we have no sin, we deceive ourselves, and the truth is not in us.* This doesn't mean that we cannot overcome sin in our lives, nor does it give an excuse to sin, as John goes on to write in a verse following: *2:1, My little children, these things write I unto you, that ye sin not. And if any man sin, we have an advocate with the Father, Jesus Christ the righteous.* As we deal with the besetting sins I want you to examine your innermost being, to ask the Lord to do as the Psalmist did in *Psa 139:23, 24, Search me, O God, and know my heart: try me, and know my thoughts: and see if there be any wicked way in me, and lead me in the way everlasting.* Again I want to say the purpose of these messages and fact sheets is not to condemn, but they are to convict us of any besetting sins that is affecting believer's lives. The condemnation will come on any who are convicted and do not repent! I am expecting to see some victories in my own life, as well as others lives, as we deal with the *'weights and besetting sins'* in our lives.

Why do I say the most important question to be asked about any thing is *'what does the Bible say about it?'*, because of what it says in *Heb 4:12,13. W*e used to sing a song when I was growing up *'There's An All-Seeing Eye Watching You'.* We tend to think of the Big Brother of government as the all-seeing eye that takes away our freedom. However, the song is talking about *'the eyes of the LORD, which run to and fro through the whole* *earth,' Zec 4:10.* There is not an unseen thing in your life that the Lord does not see

II. How does it hinder my relationship with God? Any *'weight or sin'* is *'besetting'*—causing you to be *'standing around'* and not in the race! You are out of fellowship with God when there is a *'weight or sin' y*ou are not dealing with in your life. *1 John 1: 6,7, If we say that we have fellowship with him, and walk in darkness, we lie, and do not the truth: but if we walk in the light, as he is in the light, we have fellowship one with another, and the blood of Jesus Christ his Son cleanseth us from all sin.* The bulletin by Dr. Bob Jones says, *'Walk in the light you are getting, or you will find yourself in the darkness.'* I have already given you the next verse *(v.8) If we say that we have no sin, we deceive ourselves, and the truth is not in us.* So these verses in their context are telling us to not *walk in darkness,* and that if *we walk in the light,* though we may not be sinless, *the blood of Jesus Christ his Son cleanseth us from all sin—'cleanseth'* being a continuous verb. This is not saying since I am not sinless I can sin because Jesus is going to cleanse my sin. No! *(2:1) My little children, these things write I unto you, that ye sin not.* Even in the strongest of Christians there is that *'Achilles' heel',* there is that weakness that maybe only you and the Lord know about, but don't you ever forget the devil knows where you are weak and that is where he will attack you! *"'Achilles' heel' is a fatal weakness in spite of overall strength, actually or potentially leading to downfall".* You say, *'Preacher do you think some besetting sin could actually lead to a down fall?'* Yes I do, for the Bible says, *Heb 3:1215, Take heed,* *brethren, lest there be in any of you an evil heart of unbelief, in departing from the living God. But exhort one another daily, while it is called To day; lest any of you be hardened through the deceitfulness of sin. For we are made partakers of Christ, if we hold the beginning of our confidence stedfast unto the end, while it is said, Today if ye will hear his voice, harden not your hearts, as in the provocation.*

III. How will it affect, not only my testimony, but the image of Christ and our church to others? The very word *'Christian'* means to be Christlike. *The disciples were called Christians first in Antioch, Acts 11:26.* They were called *'Christians'* because they were followers of Christ and one who follows another identifies with the one they are following. There could be a lot of subjects of *'what is wrong with . . . whatever'*, when it comes to following the world and not the Lord. I want all who come to our church to *'let your light so shine before men, that they may see your good works, and glorify your Father which is in heaven,' Mat 5:16.* Notice we do it to glorify the Father and not bring any glory to ourselves. But let me tell you, a church's image will be marred in a community when people identify themselves with the church and then live a life not pleasing to the Lord. You cannot be an effective witness for Christ if there are unconfessed and unforgiven *'weights and sins'* in your life! Paul said of those he ministered at Corinth, *Ye are our epistle written in our hearts, known and read of all men, 2 Cor 3:2.* It goes on to say, *Forasmuch as ye are manifestly declared to be the epistle of Christ, v.3.*

I know that some may think that Bro. John and I have too high standards. Robin pointed out what I have it on the pens we give to our visitors. It has the church name and address, phone number—then *Vernon Long, Pastor, He never changes (Heb.13:8)* The meaning is obviously— Jesus never changes. *Jesus Christ the same yesterday, and today, and forever.* But there is no church, there is no pastor that has as high a standard as Jesus has, for He is perfection! These verses declare we as believers are to be *epistles of Christ* and that we are *known and read of all men.* Somewhere in my files I have a poem entitled *'The Gospel According To You.'*. I remember a couple of lines in the poem that says, *'You are writing a gospel, a chapter each day, by the deeds that you do, and by the words that you say.'*

IV. Am I willing to repent of it and seek God's power, rather than my own power to overcome it? I don't know what your besetting sin is, and you don't know what my besetting sin is, but we all have one. We can go on and live our lives as if we don't. But let me say that we cannot have fellowship with the Lord as we ought to have unless we repent and turn to the Lord to overcome that which hinders us in our Christian walk. We cannot be an effective witness for Christ with any unforgiven sin in our lives. Too much of the time we try to handle the besetting sins in our way and fail to realize the power that will be ours if we deal with those little things in our lives. It tells us in *Song of Solomon 2:15* that it is *'the little foxes that spoil the vines'.* It is time we claim the promise of *1 John 4:4, Ye are of God, little children, and have overcome them: because greater is he that is in you, than he that is in the world.*

If you are unsaved, maybe you don't understand all I have said to believers today. However, I do believe you understand enough to know you are a sinner who is lost and you need to be saved.

This is the first message of 9 in the series, 'Weights and Besetting Sins,' available on the 'Monitor Messages CD.

What is Wrong With Cremation?
1 Cor 6:19, 20; Heb. 12:1, 2

1 Corinthians 6:19-20 (KJV)
¹⁹ *What? know ye not that your body is the temple of the Holy Ghost which is in you, which ye have of God, and ye are not your own?*
²⁰ *For ye are bought with a price: therefore glorify God in your body, and in your spirit, which are God's.*

Hebrews 12:1-2 (KJV)
¹ *Wherefore seeing we also are compassed about with so great a cloud of witnesses, let us lay aside every weight, and the sin which doth so easily beset us, and let us run with patience the race that is set before us,*
² *Looking unto Jesus the author and finisher of our faith; who for the joy that was set before him endured the cross, despising the shame, and is set down at the right hand of the throne of God.*

I have preached a series of 8 messages from **Heb. 12:1,2, Wherefore seeing we also are compassed about with so great a cloud of witnesses, let us lay aside every weight, and the sin which doth so easily beset us, and let us run with patience the race that is set before us, looking unto Jesus the author and finisher of our faith; who for the joy that was set before him endured the cross, despising the shame, and is set down at the right hand of the throne of God.** I was prompted, by the Spirit's direction, with Bro. Christian Powell's message at the Preaching Conference in Pigeon Forge on the besetting sins that we as believers may have in our lives. Along with the 8 messages I preached there were 5 fact sheets printed concerning: *What is wrong with body marking [tattoos] and body piercing?; A profile of the one who helps to make it easy for you to sin; What is wrong with dressing immodestly?; What is wrong with abortion?;* and *What is wrong with the new versions of the Bible?*

I encouraged you all to turn in any questions you may have about things that may be a weight or besetting sin that would hinder you in your Christian life. There have been questions and various things that prompted me to deal with a subject I am preaching about: *'What is Wrong With Cremation?'* Recently I was asked a personally question about the cremation of the body at death, though it was not turned in on one of the forms. Ada's first cousin, who is in a nursing home, was saved and he had told me, even before he was saved that he wanted me to preach his funeral. I informed him, when he was unsaved, that I would not preach him into heaven if he died lost. His sister told Ada that he was going to be cremated, so I immediately contacted his son and it was not so. Then Robin and me visited a lady recently who had told me that she wanted me to preach her funeral, and she informed that she was going to be cremated, and I told Robin that I had never preached such a memorial service and I needed to do some further study on the subject. One of my mother's sisters was cremated and me and one of my uncles [my mother's brother] went to the memorial service. We both knew that it would bother Mom to know her sister was cremated. So when she asked how my aunt looked, we got by with telling her that it was just a memorial service for my aunt. Then John mentioned in a message recently about the multitude of cremation urns found near one of the places they sacrificed children to the false god of Baal. *Jer 32:35, And they built the high places of Baal, which are in the valley of the son of Hinnom, to cause their sons and daughters to pass through the fire unto Molech.* Do you know what abortion clinics do with the mutilated bodies of babies after they take body parts and sell them? They incinerate the remaining body.

You may have a different opinion as to the cremation of our bodies at death, and I am not saying that anyone you knew who was cremated is lost forever in hell, as point 2 of the Fact Sheet says, **How does it hinder my relationship with God?** Some believe that the destruction of the body will hinder the bodily resurrection from the graves that will occur *(1 Cor 15:35-58; 1 Thes. 4:16)* which is hard to justify because you have a lot of bodies that are destroyed by fire against their will, i.e., early Christian martyrs. As well as, given enough time, each and every body decomposes to dust *(Gen. 3.19)*. Holding to the idea that 'a body must exist' limits God's power, tying His ability to the existence of a 'body'. The soul of the saved person goes to be with Christ immediately upon death *(Phil 1:23; 2 Cor 5:8; Lk 23:43)*. The soul of the lost person descends to hell immediately upon death *(Lk.16:22-23)*. That which is done to the body after death does not affect the soul's condition nor the future resurrection. However, respect for the body that the soul and the Holy Spirit resided in does concern me and others.

The purpose of this message is to share with you what I found in my study and research and why I believe cremation is wrong, though you may think differently. Because of my findings in the study I cannot consciously participate in such a memorial service where the remains are to be cremated.

In one of the attached articles it states: *Many people today are practicing the burning of human bodies after death for emotional reasons (to shorten the grieving process), economical reasons (much less expensive) and ecological reasons (to save valuable land). By the year 2010 some estimate that 34% of all Americans will be cremated. This is an alarming statistic. We must remember that economic reasons do not override the timeless ethical principles in the Bible concerning this matter of cremation.* The funeral home that took care of Cindy's funeral offered a cheaper burial plan, using cremation. I hope you will read the fact sheet I prepared on the subject and will read the other numerous articles that are available, if you have any questions about it.

I was reminded in Bro Ronnie Williamson's article of an incident that happened a few years ago in Georgia. He wrote: More than 300 corpses stacked in sheds or rotting in the woods were found. This certainly was a nightmare for the many families involved. The criminal investigation in Lafayette, Georgia, of this bizarre story surrounded a crematory. Originally, the excuse for the decomposing bodies was a broken incinerator. However, that was not true and photos of the bodies were found on the office computer of Ray Brent Marsh, the crematory's operators. Think about this, hundreds of bodies to be cremated - this service was paid for by the deceased family.

There was a funeral home there in Milldale, TN close to the church Cindy attended that back some years ago they were taking the bodies out of the caskets and burying them, then reselling the caskets. Obviously, they didn't have respect for the bodies of the deceased.

To give credit where credit is due, so that I will not be accused of plagiarizing, I want to use the outline and article in March, 2007 issue of The Baptist Challenge, entitled, 'What Does The Bible Say About Cremation?' by Garner Smith.

He writes, as stated in the fact sheet, There are two known cases of cremation in the Bible. In *Josh.7:25-26* it is used of Achan as a method of judgment of God not the disposing of a body. In *1 Sam.31:8-13* again it is not used as a means of burial or disposing of a body but for special purposes to keep from further misuse of the body. The people graciously chose to burn the bodies of Saul and his sons out of respect for their bodies in view of the humiliation and disgraceful acts that the Philistines were performing with their bodies. However, we see the people still honoring the practice of burial since they buried their bones under the tree. We must then conclude that the practice of even burning the flesh of God's people was not a normal practice. It was evidently done in rare cases when the body was disgraced and mutilated beyond recognition or more specifically, in this case, when the heathen people were desecrating the human body by terrible acts of dishonor. This text in no way supports the practice of cremation. It was merely a respectful way to honor the dead bodies that had been mutilated beyond recognition and disgraced among a wicked heathen society. But none of this was a common practice. It was simply a necessary practice for unique circumstances and times. Cremation was not a Hebrew or Scriptural custom.

Over and over again in the Bible God commands the burning of things as a sign of displeasure and a dishonorable way of disposing of a body. When God commands cremation it is a severe form of contempt or punishment, not a normal, honorable, or respectful means of disposing of a body.

I do not believe a Christian should use cremation as a means for disposing of the body because of the following reasons:

(1) It is of heathen or pagan origin and practice. The Romans copied it from the Greeks and it was common in pagan Europe until the growth of Christianity, then it

declined. The reason paganism practiced cremation was to prevent the use of the body by evil spirits or for magic ceremonies.

(2) It is against Scripture. When we bury a body in the ground we are following the commands of God. The body is to return to the earth from whence it was made. This is done in a natural way as ordained by God *(Gen. 3:19)*. God Himself set the example in His own burying of the body of Moses *(Deut. 34:5-6)*.

(3) We have Christ's example in opposition to cremation. In God's plan of redemption part of that plan was Christ was to be buried *(Matt. 12:38-40; 1 Cor. 15:3-4)*.

(4) The burial of the body was practiced by God's faithful Old Testament saints. In *Genesis 23:4* we see Abraham seeking a burial place for his wife. If cremation was acceptable why go to so much trouble to bury her?

(5) The sanctity of the human body. Christian's bodies belong to the Lord

(1 Cor. 6:19-20). We were *'fearfully and wonderfully made' (Psa 139:14)* in our mother's womb and I can't imagine taking that body at death and destroying it by the fires of a crematory. *W*e will be observing *'Sanctity of Life Sunday'* January 18. Our bodies are the instruments used by God while we are here on earth *(Rom. 6:13)*. Our bodies should be buried in such a way to proclaim our faith in the sure and certain hope of the resurrection. *Romans 14:8* says that when we die we are to die unto the

Lord. Our death and burial should declare Gods ownership of our body and glorify Him. We as Christians are not free to do with our bodies as we will. We are God's and must consider and do His will in all things.

Because of the aforementioned reasons we must conclude the practice of cremation should never be practiced by a Christian. It has no support from the Scripture and was rejected by both Israel and the early Christians. It was considered a heathen custom and a judgment of God. It dishonors the body and seeks to deny the resurrection. Christian burial is a necessary part of our Christian faith from beginning to end and to forsake it is to forsake our God-given faith.

In the lengthy 13 page discussion of cremation, *'What About Cremation'* by Kelly Sensenig, he gives the following reasons why Christians should not be cremated: because of the heathen practice of cremation; because the burning of a body was the sign of God's judgment and wrath; because God practices burial; because of their belief in the future resurrection; because God's people have always practiced burial; and because Jesus was not cremated.

As stated in the Fact Sheet, I offer this suggestion: Your responsibility, even in death, is to honor God by sending the world a lasting testimony of your faith in God's resurrection program! Arrange your funeral plans ahead of time and be prepared to honor God's Word and the resurrection program of our Lord through burial. Practice burial, as God's people have always practiced, so that you might outwardly demonstrate your own faith as a Christian in God's resurrection program from our earthly temple. The Lord Jesus Christ was buried, and He is our great example (see *John 19:38-42)*. But that is not the rest of the story, for we see when the women came to the tomb on the third day the angels said to them, *Why seek ye the living among the dead? He is not here, but is risen, Luke 24:5,6.*

I don't know all I understand about the planting of my body in the ground, but I do know what the Bible says about it in *1 Cor 15:35-58.*

This is the final message of 9 in the series, 'Weights and Besetting Sins,' available on the 'Monitor Messages CD. The messages are in conjunction with the 6 'Facts Sheets,' listed below, along with the other messages in the series.

What is wrong with body marking [tattoos] and body piercing?
- Fact Sheet 1
A profile of the one who helps to make it easy for you to sin
- Fact Sheet 2
What is wrong with dressing immodestly?
- Fact Sheet 3
What is wrong with abortion?
- Fact Sheet 4
What is wrong with the new versions of the Bible?'
- Fact Sheet 5
What is wrong with Cremation?
– Fact Sheet 6

Words of Anguish
Matt.27:32-46

32 And as they came out, they found a man of Cyrene, Simon by name: him they compelled to bear his cross.

33 And when they were come unto a place called Golgotha, that is to say, a place of a skull,

34 They gave him vinegar to drink mingled with gall: and when he had tasted thereof, he would not drink.

35 And they crucified him, and parted his garments, casting lots: that it might be fulfilled which was spoken by the prophet, They parted my garments among them, and upon my vesture did they cast lots.

36 And sitting down they watched him there;

37 And set up over his head his accusation written, THIS IS JESUS THE KING OF THE JEWS.

38 Then were there two thieves crucified with him, one on the right hand, and another on the left.

39 And they that passed by reviled him, wagging their heads,

40 And saying, Thou that destroyest the temple, and buildest it in three days, save thyself. If thou be the Son of God, come down from the cross.

41 Likewise also the chief priests mocking him, with the scribes and elders, said,

42 He saved others; himself he cannot save. If he be the King of Israel, let him now come down from the cross, and we will believe him.

43 He trusted in God; let him deliver him now, if he will have him: for he said, I am the Son of God.

44 The thieves also, which were crucified with him, cast the same in his teeth.

45 Now from the sixth hour there was darkness over all the land unto the ninth hour.

46 And about the ninth hour Jesus cried with a loud voice, saying, Eli, Eli, lama sabachthani? that is to say, My God, my God, why hast thou forsaken me?

This is the 4th saying that Jesus uttered from the cross. It stands in the center of the seven and seems almost fitting that it should be so, for here the tragedy of the crucifixion reached its climax. The first three sayings concerned others, these final four concerns Himself. Of all the sayings I suppose this one is the hardest to fully understand in our finite minds. Spurgeon-*'Fully understand it, who can? I felt when I read these words that they seemed to say, 'you cannot preach from us.'* I have come to more fully understand what he meant, as I've studied for this message. As I studied for the other messages I did realize more fully the meaning of each; when He cried, **Father, forgive them for they know not** *what they do;* I identified myself with that saying, for I too was once blinded by the god of this world, until *the light shined out of darkness into my heart giving light of the knowledge of Christ, 2 Cor.4:6.* As He said to the repent-ant thief, *Verily I say unto thee, today thou shalt be with me in paradise,* I saw His amazing saving grace being manifested, for the thief could do nothing to merit salvation, as his hands and feet were now nailed to the cross, but he could do all that was necessary to be saved. Though he couldn't move his hands and feet, his heart could be moved and he still had the use of his tongue -*Rom.10:10, For with the heart man believeth unto righteousness; and with the mouth confession is made unto salvation.* If anyone is ever saved *its by grace thru faith. not of works(Eph.2:8,9)* If you're depending upon something you've done to merit salvation, then you don't have the salvation and forgiveness the Bible teaches. Last week when I preached on *Woman, behold thy Son,* then He said to John, *Behold thy mother,* we can in a sense understand their affection to Him and His affection to them, and most importantly I hope you saw His affection for us. But when we come to this statement. *My God, My God, why hast Thou forsaken me?,* it becomes difficult for us to comprehend.

Though it is beyond our comprehension to fully understand this saying, there are some things we can understand about it, and that is what I want you to see in this message: 3 hours have elapsed since He has said anything; that Jesus felt forsaken is beyond question, which came about in part through His physical torture. Let us not forget that Jesus was a man, just as we are. Torture weakens the whole man. He had suffered terribly. . Endured 4 mock trials before Annas, Caiphas, Herod and Pilate . . Scourged, crowned with a crown of thorns . . went thru the suffering related in previous messages . . now he's been upon the cross for almost 6 hrs. It is not surprising that His physical suffering had taken its toll in some measure upon His vivid sense of God. The full reason why Jesus came to feel Himself forsaken is, I repeat, beyond our understanding. On the cross he was made *'sin for us, who knew no sin' 2 Cor 5:21.* He did not give up and call 12 legions of angels*(Mat.26:53)*, but He did turn to God the Father in prayer, with the only question Jesus ever addressed to God, a prayer offered in faith, with conviction that God was still His very own-*My God,* He prayed. As long as we can claim God as our very own, we cannot be utterly desolate. Not only did Jesus pray in faith that God was still His very own, but He prayed in faith that God knew the answer to this perplexing question and that in love He would give Him the answer *(Matt.27:32-46).*

What can we understand from this saying and what does it help us see?

I. We see the awfulness of sin and its wages-*The wages of sin is death Rom.6: 23.* What is death? What is *Rom.6:23* talking about? What does *Rom.5:12* say? *Wherefore, as by one man sin entered into the world, and death by sin; and so death passed upon all men, for that all have sinned.* Had there been no sin there would have been no death. What is death? When we hear the word *'death'* we usually think of death of this body we live in, and certainly that is a part of the curse of sin. Physical death, which we all must suffer, unless the

Lord comes in our lifetime, is the separation of the soul from the body. *Eccl 12:7, Then shall the dust return to the earth as it was: and the spirit shall return unto God who gave it.* Man is different from all of God's creation in that we have an eternal living soul—we were created in the image of God. Man is different, we die the physical death like other animal life--*Eccl 3:19,20 For that which befalleth the sons of men befalleth beasts; even one thing befalleth them: as the one dieth, so dieth the other; yea, they have all one breath; so that a man hath no preeminence above a beast: for all is vanity. All go unto one place; all are of the dust, and all turn to dust again;* but listen to the next verse, *Eccl 3:21 Who knoweth the spirit of man that goeth upward, and the spirit of the beast that goeth downward to the earth?*

When the Bible speaks of death, there is a 2nd death recorded in *Rev 20:14,15, And death and hell were cast into the lake of fire. This is the second death. And whosoever was not found written in the book of life was cast into the lake of fire.* Also in *Rev 21:8 But the fearful, and unbelieving, and the abominable, and murderers, and whoremongers, and sorcerers, and idolaters, and all liars, shall have their part in the lake which burneth with fire and brim-stone: which is the second death.* If your name is not recorded in the Book of Life when you die your physical death, you will suffer this death as well. When it says to us in *1 Th 5:9,10a, For God hath not appointed us to wrath, but to obtain salvation by our Lord Jesus Christ, Who died for us,* it is talking about more than His physical death on Calvary's cross, but includes the 2nd death, that every last one of us deserve to suffer. During those 3 hrs, as the sun refused to shine, we see the awfulness of sin and its wages-*Luke 23:44 And it was about the sixth hour, and there was a darkness over all the earth until the ninth hour.* The physical death was an agonizing death, as I've related how the spikes were driven in His hands and feet, after He had been scourged, buffeted and mocked. But His forsaking by God caused more anguish than anything they had done to His body thus far. His physical death was a result of His being rejected by man, but now we see Him being rejected and forsaken by God. Why? Because He was bearing *our sins in his own body on the tree, (I Pt.2:24)* He had taken our place and was suffering for our sins, *the just for the unjust, that He might bring us to God (I Pt.3:18)* In our finite minds we cannot comprehend how the infinite God-man Jesus Christ, could suffer all the eternity of eternal separation from God. But thank God, He did and by trusting Him, my name is recorded in the Book of Life through the shed blood of Jesus Christ. God turned His back on Jesus for my sake, Jesus satisfied the penalty for my sin and any who abide in Him do not have the penalty of the 2nd death awaiting them-**Rev 20:6**, *Blessed and holy is he that hath part in the first resurrection: on such the second death hath no power.* An awful doom awaits the lost--*2 Th 1:8,9, In flaming fire taking vengeance on them that know not God, and that obey not the gospel of our Lord Jesus Christ: who shall be punished with everlasting destruction from the presence of the Lord, and from the glory of his power.* The agony of the physical pain on the cross was terrible, but the real anguish of suffering was when Jesus cried, *My God, My God, Why hast Thou forsaken me? T*he physical agonies of hell will be terrible, but the real agony and anguish of the unbeliever throughout all eternity will be the eternal separation from God, with no hope of reconciliation. Jesus said of the rich man in *Luke 16:26 And beside all this, between us and you there is a great gulf fixed: so that they which would pass from hence to you cannot; neither can they pass to us, that would come from thence.*

I hope and pray that you have comprehended to some degree the awfulness of sin and its wages. What it costs Christ to have God turn His back on Him, and that it will cost you eternal separation from God in an eternal hell, if you do not accept Jesus payment for your sins.

What else can we understand from this saying and what does it help us see?

II. We see the absolute holiness of God and His inflexible justice. The tragedy of Calvary must be viewed from at least 4 different viewpoints for us to understand what Christ did for us, who deserve not only the physical death like He suffered, but the second death (eternal separation from God) as well. What are these 4 viewpoints?

1. At the cross man did a work; he displayed his depravity by taking the Perfect One and with wicked hands nailed Him to a cross.

2. At the cross Satan did a work: he manifested his enmity against the woman's seed by bruising His heel as prophesied in *Gen.3:15.*

3. At the cross the Lord Jesus did a work: *He died the just for the unjust, that He might bring us to God, I Pet.3:18.*

4. At the cross God did a work: He exhibited His

holiness and satisfied His justice by pouring out His wrath on the One Who was made sin for us.

His justice by pouring out His wrath on the One Who was made sin for us. If there is any stronger Scripture on the holiness of God than when He turned His back on Jesus, I don't know where it is. So holy is God that we are told in *Hab 1:13, Thou art of purer eyes than to behold evil, and canst not look on iniquity.* It was because the Saviour was bearing our sins that the thrice holy God would not so much as look on Him, He turned His face from Him and forsook Him. Because He was enduring sin's terrific judgment, He was forsaken of God. God's holy character could do no less than judge sin, even though it be found on Christ Himself. At the cross then, God's justice was satisfied and His holiness vindicated. That's why Jesus cried, *My God, My God, Why hast thou forsaken me?*

What else can we understand from this saying and what does it help us see?

III. We see the basis for our salvation. God is holy and therefore cannot look upon sin. God is just and therefore He judges sin wherever it is found, but God is love as well: *God delighteth in mercy (Micah 7:18)* and therefore infinite wisdom devised a way whereby justice might be satisfied and mercy left free to flow out to guilty sinners. This way was the way of substitution, the Just suffering for the unjust. At the cross our iniquities were laid upon Christ and therefore did our divine judgment fall upon Him. There was no way of transferring sin without also transferring its penalty. The death of Christ upon the cross was death of a curse--*Gal 3:13, Christ hath redeemed us from the curse of the law, being made a curse for us: for it is written, Cursed is every one that hangeth on a tree.* The curse of sin is death— spiritual death, the 2nd death, or alienation from God.

This is apparent from the words of Christ, which He will speak in the future judgment-*Mat 25:41, Then shall he say also unto them on the left hand, Depart from me, ye cursed, into everlasting fire, pre-pared for the devil and his angels.* Even in Isaiah's day we find that hell had to be enlarged, now nearly 3000 yrs later, we see iniquity abounding as never before and perhaps hell has enlarged even more--*Isa 5:14-16 Therefore hell hath enlarged herself, and opened her mouth without measure: and their glory, and their multitude, and their pomp, and he that rejoiceth, shall descend into it. And the mean man shall be brought down, and the mighty man shall be humbled, and the eyes of the lofty shall be humbled: but the LORD of hosts shall be exalted in judgment, and God that is holy shall be sanctified in righteousness.* Listen to *Isa 14:9-11 Hell from beneath is moved for thee to meet thee at thy coming: it stirreth up the dead for thee, even all the chief ones of the earth; it hath raised up from their thrones all the kings of the nations. All they shall speak and say unto thee, Art thou also become weak as we? art thou become like unto us? Thy pomp is brought down to the grave, and the noise of thy viols: the worm is spread under thee, and the worms cover thee.* Hell not only proves the justice of God, but His holiness and righteousness, as well. But Christ took our curse of eternal suffering and alienation from God because of our sins, and therefore He cried,

My God, My God, Why hast thou forsaken me?

What else can we understand from this saying and what does it help us see?

IV. We see the judgment of God on sin. The cry of the Saviour foretells the final condition of every lost soul—forsaken of God. If I am a faithful preacher of the Word, it compels me to warn you of the false teachings of our day. We are told by the liberals that God loves everybody and that He is too merciful to ever carry out the judgment proclaimed in His Word. Don't you believe old Satan's lie like Eve did and got us into the mess we are in. God had said concerning the tree of knowledge of good and evil in the Garden of Eden-*In the day thou eatest thereof thou shalt surely die(Gen.2:17)* The serpent said, *Ye shall not surely die(3:4).* But whose word was proven true? Not the devil's, for he was *a liar and the father of it (John 8:44)* You know what happened, our first parents died spiritually the day they disobeyed the command of God. One day, every unsaved person who dies in their sin will suffer the agony that Christ suffered as He was forsaken by God on the cross. God says sin must be judged, He extends His mercy today, as He has provided a Saviour who has been judged and suffered for our sins. There is no limit to God's mercy this side of eternity and *He is not willing that any should perish, but that all should come to repentance(2 Pet.5:9) Acts 17:30,31 And the times of this ignorance God winked at; but now commandeth all men everywhere to repent: because he hath* *appointed a day, in the which he will judge the world in righteousness by that man whom he hath ordained; whereof he hath given assurance unto all men, in that he hath raised him from the dead.*

The day of mercy will one day end for those who continue to reject Christ. *Heb 9:27, And as it is appointed unto men once to die, but after this the judgment.* In the Day of Judgment God will deal in justice, not mercy. He will one day avenge the mercy you have scorned. Because He is holy and just God must judge sin, wherever it is found. If God *"spared not His own Son, but delivered Him up for us all (Rom.8:32),* what possible hope is there for the sinner that He will spare you when you stand before Him at the Great White Throne Judgement. The Word of Truth is explicit- *John 3:36, He that believeth on the Son hath everlasting life: and he that believeth not the Son shall not see life; but the wrath of God abideth on him.* If you die in your sins, you will be judged for your sins. Listen again to *2 Th 1:8,9, In flaming fire taking vengeance on them that know not God, and that obey not the gospel of our Lord Jesus Christ: who shall be punished with everlasting destruction from the presence of the Lord, and from the glory of his power;* but *v.10* says, *When he shall come to be glorified in his saints, and to be admired in all them that believe (because our testimony among you was believed) in that day.*

Those by the cross failed to understand what He said *(Matt.27:47-49).* Maybe we cannot fully comprehend the real depth of the meaning of *My God, my God, why hast thou forsaken me?* But I believe you can see the awfulness of sin and its wages; the absolute holiness of God and His inflexible justice; the basis for our salvation; and the judgment of God on sin.

In the bulletin I've reprinted a devotion which I read from the *Days of Praise* devotion book on February 11, which says the following of the *'ninth hour.'*

The Ninth Hour

And about the ninth hour Jesus cried with a loud voice, saying, Eli, Eli, lama sabachthani? That is to say. My God, my God. Why hast thou forsaken me? (Matthew 27:46).

At the apex of the sufferings of the Lamb of God for the sins of the world, it was fitting that He should utter this desolate cry at the ninth hour, for this was the time of the regular evening sacrifice, as well as the time of evening prayers, among the people of ancient Israel.

It was at this hour that Elijah prayed to God against the prophets of Baal on Mount Carmel, and God answered by fire from heaven *(I Kings 18:36-39).* This was also the hour of Ezra's great prayer of confession and intercession *(Ezra 9:5),* followed by a wonderful revival among the backslidden people of Israel. When Daniel uttered his own prayer of confession and intercession *'about the time of the evening oblation' (Daniel 9:21),* God sent the angel Gabriel to answer his prayer. In the New Testament. *'Peter and John went up together into the temple at the hour of prayer, being the ninth hour' (Acts 3:1),* and the result was the first apostolic miracle. The first Gentile convert to Christ was Cornelius, who was praying *'about the ninth hour of the day' (Acts 10:3)* when he, like Daniel, received a visit from an angel of God to tell him to send for Peter, who would lead him to Christ.

In all recorded instances of prayer at the ninth hour, at the daily evening sacrifice, God answered the prayer in a marvelous way. But when the Lord Jesus Christ prayed, God did not answer, for He had forsaken His own Son. *'Why?'* He cried, but He knew, and now we know that it was simply because He *'loved me. And gave Himself for me' (Galatians 2:20).* The measure of His love is the cross and separation from the Father, *'that He by the grace of God should taste death for every man' (Hebrews 2:9).* This is why He died!

Yes, the measure of His love for us is not only the physical death He suffered for us, but also our second death, which is separation from God for eternity. In this message you have seen the justice, mercy and grace of God as it applies to us: Justice is when you get what you deserve; mercy is when you don't get what you deserve; and grace is when you get what you don't deserve.

This is the fourth of 7 message of the series, 'The Last Words of Christ From the Cross,' available on the 'Monitor Messages' CD.

Wherein Have We Robbed Thee?
Mal.3:8-12

8 Will a man rob God? Yet ye have robbed me. But ye say, Wherein have we robbed thee? In tithes and offerings.

9 Ye are cursed with a curse: for ye have robbed me, even this whole nation.

10 Bring ye all the tithes into the storehouse, that there may be meat in mine house, and prove me now herewith, saith the LORD of hosts, if I will not open you the windows of heaven, and pour you out a blessing, that there shall not be room enough to receive it.

11 And I will rebuke the devourer for your sakes, and he shall not destroy the fruits of your ground; neither shall your vine cast her fruit before the time in the field, saith the LORD of hosts.

12 And all nations shall call you blessed: for ye shall be a delightsome land, saith the LORD of hosts.

When I started the stewardship series in **Malachi,** perhaps you thought I was going to preach a series on tithing. Most folks when you say you are going to preach on stewardship think you are referring to money and people who know the Word are familiar with **Mal.3:8-12.** But in preparing for these messages I have found in my word study of **'wherein'** **t**here are many other stewardship responsibilities found in **Malachi.** As I have preached on the stewardship of our love to God, **Wherein hast thou loved me?(1:2)** love must be the basis of all we give to the Lord; I preached on the stewardship of our worship-**Wherein have we polluted Thee? (1:7); Wherein have we wearied Him? (2:17);** and last Sunday evening I preached from **3:7, Wherein shall we return?** --pointing out the need to repent and quit excusing sin. **We** come now to this 6th **'wherein' Wherein have we robbed Thee?'** People are robbing God in more ways than just in their giving, as you will see in the message.

I had never seen this passage in the light that I want to relate it to you. They may have been giving 10% to other charities or giving to help someone else in need, but they were not following God's prescribed method and were not bringing **all the tithes t**o the temple. I pointed out in the message on worship-**'Wherein have we polluted Thee?' th**ey were offering the blind, the lame, and sick for sacrifice. Their place of worship was the storehouse to which they were to bring all the tithes. The storehouse was a series of compartments in the temple area where they gathered food to take care of the priests and needs of others. Do you know where the New Testament storehouse is? The church-*Upon the first day of the week let every one of you lay by him in store, as God hath prospered him, that there be no gatherings when I come1 Cor 16:2.* Where are we to be on *the first day of the week?* In church! The Greek word translated *'store' he*re is an exact translation of the Hebrew word translated *'storehouse' in Mal.3:10.* What I want to bring out in this message has been covered in the previous messages. If we love God like we should there will not only be *thanksgiving bu*t there will also be *thanksliving. 'Wherein shall we return?'* If you're not living a life of *thanksliving I* hope you will recognize your need for repentance-*1 John 1:8, 9, If we say that we have no sin, we deceive ourselves, and the truth is not in us. If we confess our sins, he is faithful and just to forgive us our sins, and to cleanse us from all unrighteousness. Ha*ving said all this about *thanksliving li*sten to what God says about our *thanksgiving.*

One of the most blessed services we had in our mission work in Jackson, TN was a Sunday we designated *'Trade Places With God' Sunday.* We as pastor and church board first agreed that we would commit to giving 90% on the set Sunday in order to pay our church bonds off by Jan., 1988, and started earlier in the year laying aside so we could meet our goal. We not only paid off our church bonds, but also all our insurance premiums in advance for the coming year. My message that Sunday was. *'It All Belongs To Him' a*nd my text was *1 Chr 29:14, But who am I, and what is my people, that we should be able to offer so willingly after this sort? for all things come of thee, and of thine own have we given thee.* I have shared that with you to say what I want to say today about not just the 10%, but the 90% you have, it all belongs to God!.

I. What does the Bible say about our 'thanks*giving?' Preachers fail to preach in the area of people's financial support of the church because many times they fear they will be accused of preaching for money. Even though I myself don't preach about it that much, its in the Bible and we ought not fail to preach it, even though some may accuse us wrongly. The accusers will be those who are not giving as they should to the ministries of the church.

A. The Bible does say where we are to give to the work of the Lord. It is the *'storehouse.'* *It* is to be at the place where we gather with other believers to worship the Lord. Our tithes are not to be sent off to some TV or radio preacher, but are to be given through the local church. It is not wrong to support TV and radio programs that preach the Gospel, but they are not to receive the tithe, nor even a portion of it--*Mal 3:10, Bring ye all the tithes into the storehouse.* Listen again to *1 Cor 16:2, Upon the first day of the week let every one of you lay by him in store, as God hath prospered him, that there be no gatherings when I come.* *'Christian Family's Stewardship' is* a topic *I* have spoken on in Family Life Conferences and I point out from this verse that it not only tells us where and when we are to give, but also who is to give--*'every one of you.'* It tells us to give proportionally *'as God hath prospered.'* *If* we gave as God has prospered it would be far more than just 10% of what He has blessed us with. In America we have been prospered like no other people; therefore, we have a greater obligation than the less fortunate. J. C. Penney was a believer who practiced giving as God prospered him and by the time his death he *'traded places with God'* giving 90% of his income to religious and charitable causes. I'm not saying as some, who will try to get you to send them money that you will receive tenfold if you give. I am saying, if you prove God, as our text says and give, that you will receive *'a blessing, that there shall not be room enough to receive it.'*—not necessarily material blessings. We should give to the Lord's work, not so we will receive material blessings, but so we will be blessed and receive spiritual blessings that I will speak on tonight. *Remember the words of the Lord Jesus, how he said, It is more blessed to give than to receive, Acts 20:35.*

II. We also find out how we should give? *(2 Cor 9:7)* **Th**e grace of giving ought to be exercised as an act of worship with preparation, purpose, and joy. Giving that is reluctant or coerced is not pleasing to God, **for God loves a cheerful [hilaros, Gk.] giver.** We are warned about giving **grudgingly;** there is no joy in this attitude, but only sorrow as one is forced or embarrassed into giving. When a person gets a calculator out to see to the penny what his tithe is, it says to me that he is giving out of necessity when he writes his check for $48.94. Paul instructs the believer to give **'bountifully' (2 Cor 9:6).** **Pe**ople will *'pledge' to* give to missions over a period of time, when an emotional appeal is given by the missionary; but when the time for giving comes, there is no joy. That is why missionaries have to raise more than twice as much for their support, as our mission boards know that many will not continue to give as they have *'pledged.'*

III. What about the stewardship of the 90%? Does God only hold us accountable for the tithe? All of us know that ***Mal.3:10 te***lls us to bring *'all the tithes into the storehouse,' as* I just read it. Jesus put His approval upon tithing--*Mt 23:23 Woe unto you, scribes and Pharisees, hypocrites! For ye pay tithe of mint and anise and cummin, and have omitted the weightier matters of the law, judgment, mercy, and faith: these ought ye to have done, and not to leave the other undone. Je*sus challenges the Pharisees' failure to observe judgment and love in the law; whereas, on the other hand, He affirms their practice of tithing even insignificant garden vegetables. The full revelation of God in the N.T. reveals that we are to practice 100% stewardship. All we have belongs to God and should be used for His glory and according to His dictates. Tithing is only the beginning place of Christian stewardship, not the end. God does not want you to give less than a tithe, but He may want you to give much more through His enabling grace, as you have been blessed abundantly. .

I get the feeling that many think once the 10% is out of the way, the rest is theirs, scot-free, to do with as they please. God is not so much trying to teach us fractions as to get us to understand that it all belongs to Him-the $9 as well as the $1 in the collection plate. In their concern to be biblical, many overlook the fact that stewardship has something to say not only about the 10% but about the other 90%. After all, that's where we do a significant part of our living--in the 90%. It is where we reveal what we think is important. It is in the 90%, not in the 10%, that we publicly and conspicuously witness to what we really believe are the priorities of discipleship. That is the main emphasis I want to make in this message.

IV. Discipleship [thanksliving] in the 90% of your living is much more important in the work of God than your tithe. What good would it do to have a church full who gave 50% of all they had and yet would not lift a finger to sing, to pray, to teach, to preach? It would be a rather dull service if all we did was take the offering and sit around and wait for someone to do something. What good would it do the church if everyone gave to help the church grow and then no one would go out and try to reach others for Jesus? Are you giving so others can go and not going yourself? Jesus said, *Go ye into all the world, and preach the gospel to every creature, Mark 16:15.* Jesus said there are more important things than tithing--*the weightier matters of the law, judgment, mercy, and faith: these ought ye to have done, and not to leave the other undone.* Th*e*re are 2 verses I share with you from *Hosea--4:1, the Lord hath a controversy with the inhabitants of the land, because there is no truth, nor mercy, nor knowledge of God in the land; 6:6, For I desired mercy, and not sacrifice; and the knowledge of God more than burnt offerings.*

The message is about robbing God--*Wherein have we robbed Thee?* God still feels that *truth, mercy and knowledge o*f God in the land are more important than sacrificial offerings-*these ought ye to have done, and not to leave the other undone.* He wants you in His service and not sitting around giving and then doing nothing about His Great Commission of reaching others for Christ. Listen again to *Mal 3:10, Bring ye all the tithes into the storehouse, that there may be meat in mine house, and prove me now herewith, saith the LORD of hosts, if I will not open you the windows of heaven, and pour you out a blessing, that there shall not be room enough to receive it.. Th*is applies to your giving [thanksgiving], as well as your living [thanksliving]. Prove the Lord by giving your life—your time and your talents to His use. I say on the authority of God's Word, you will be blessed by God if you will do more for the Lord. God will use you where He cannot use me or anyone else, you are a unique individual. *1 Cor 4:7, For who maketh thee to differ from another? and what hast thou that thou didst not receive? now if thou didst receive it, why dost thou glory, as if thou hadst not received it?* I want you to consider what Paul said in *2 Tim 2:6,7, The husbandman that laboureth must be first partaker of the fruits. Consider what I say; and the Lord give thee understanding in all things. I* preach this message for your benefit, for *it is more blessed to give than to receive.* As one preacher answered one who said, *'I can't afford to tithe.' He* told the person, *'You can't afford not to tithe.'*

To the unsaved I want to say that God wants you to realize that He made you like you are. You too have a stewardship responsibility of your eternal soul. I hope you too have understood what I have said in the message. God is not as near concerned about what you may be able to give, as He is about you giving your life to Him today. Don't let the devil try to tell you that I just preached on money today! No, I have said the most important thing that you or anyone else can do is to give your life and soul to the Lord. If you are a sinner and leave this service unsaved you will refuse the greatest payment that has ever been given to God, and that was the life of His Son, Jesus Christ as a payment for your sins. He suffered in your behalf so that you will not have to spend an eternity in hell. The price He paid for your sins was not silver and gold, but His precious blood. Listen to *1 Pet 1:18-21; Rom 10:9.*

This is the fourth message of the series 9 messages from the 'Malachi Stewardship,' series available on the 'Monitor Messages' and the 'Stewardship Messages' CD.

Vernon Long | 199
Monitor Messages

The Unpardonable Sin
1 John 5:16, 17; Mat 12:31, 32

1 John 5:16-17

16 If any man see his brother sin a sin which is not unto death, he shall ask, and he shall give him life for them that sin not unto death. There is a sin unto death: I do not say that he shall pray for it.

17 All unrighteousness is sin: and there is a sin not unto death.

Matthew 12:31-32

31 Wherefore I say unto you, All manner of sin and blasphemy shall be forgiven unto men: but the blasphemy against the Holy Ghost shall not be forgiven unto men.

32 And whosoever speaketh a word against the Son of man, it shall be forgiven him: but whosoever speaketh against the Holy Ghost, it shall not be forgiven him, neither in this world, neither in the world to come.

In the expository messages I preach in different books of the Bible, as I feel led of the Holy Spirit, I also preach some topical messages.

In this series of messages from **1ˢᵗ John** most of them have been expository, i.e., a verse by verse preaching of the Word. I came to our text in **1 John 5:16,17** *an*d recalled a message I preached in Jackson, TN in Aug. '82 and in Jan.'95 at Leadington MO. The message is *'The Unpardonable Sin',* from a series of 27 messages I preached on the Holy Spirit and the text for the message is ***Mat 12:31,32.*** In the series I preached on several sins against the Holy Ghost—grieving or vexing, quenching, lying to, tempting, resisting, defiling our bodies (the temple of the H. G.), defiling the body of organized believers. All of these sins mentioned are forgivable sins against the Spirit of God, but continual sin in any of these areas may lead one to commit the unpardonable sin, for which there is no forgiveness. When I preached the series through the Free Will Baptist Treatise and came to the chapter on *'Perseverance of the Saints';* I preached two messages concerning apostasy, *'Forfeiting God's Promises' a*nd *'Can a Child of God Be Lost?'*

I will be using many Scriptures which deal with the subject of apostasy, and the unpardonable sin. I encourage you to take notes of the verses for further study on your own, as I will read the Scriptures as printed in my outline.

I realize the subject of the unpardonable sin is a difficult subject. You may ask **then why do I deal with such a subject?** Basically two reasons: **1) It is in the Bible.** God thought it was important enough to be in the Bible and even though some subjects in the Bible may be popular or unpopular, pleasant or unpleasant, easy to understand or difficult, God says that I am to preach the whole counsel of God; **2) It is a solemn warning to all who will continue to live in sin.** I know there is much misunderstanding concerning our text. There are those who say the unpardonable sin is some definite act the sinner does, and there are those who make it a *'state of the soul'* to which one may arrive. Though these views differ, I hope in this message I can show the same truth which both teach. *In arriving at this truth I want to answer three questions: Is it possible to commit an unpardonable sin? What is it? Who can commit it?*

I. Is it possible to commit the unpardonable sin? To answer that question we must look in the Book and not rely upon human reasoning. The Bible says it is possible to commit such a sin *(Mat 12:31,32). Gen. 6:3, My Spirit shall not always strive with man. (Num.15:30,31; Heb.l0:26)* Did you know that prayers for those who have committed such a sin will go unheard, which is further proof that it is possible to commit such a sin *(Jer.7:16; 11:14; 14:10,11).* It seems that God had given these people up and told Jeremiah not to even pray for them. They had reached the hopeless state for which there is no remedy, as those mentioned in our text in *1 John 5:16.* John Gill's Commentary says of *v.16--There is a sin unto death; which is not only deserving of death, as every other sin is, but which certainly and inevitably issues in death in all that commit it, without exception; and that is the sin against the Holy Ghost, which is neither forgiven in this world nor in that to come, and therefore must be unto death; it is a sinning willfully, not in a practical, but doctrinal way, after a man has received the knowledge of the truth; it is a willful denial of the truth of the Gospel, particularly that peace, pardon, righteousness,* *eternal life, and salvation, are by Jesus Christ, contrary to the light of his mind, and this joined with malice and obstinacy; so that there is no more or other sacrifice for such a sin; there is nothing but a fearful looking for of wrath and fury to fall on such opposers of the way of life; and as the presumptuous sinners under Moses's law died without mercy, so must these despiteful ones under the Gospel.*

II. What is the unpardonable sin? Is it a definite act of sin or is it a state of the soul to which one may arrive? Let's first look at—

A. What it is not—It is not the sin of adultery, or fornication as some teach. *(1 Cor. 6:15-20)* There is pardon for the scarlet sin—in **John 4 C**hrist gave the living water to the woman of Samaria; and the woman taken in adultery by the scribes and Pharisees, Christ said to her in **John 8:11, Neither do I condemn thee: go and sin no more.** Murder in the minds of some is beyond forgiveness, even though the murderer's life is taken by capital punishment and he pays the civil penalty for his crime as prescribed in **Gen. 6:9, Whoso sheddeth man's blood, by man shall his blood be shed: for in the image of God made He man—s**ome believe a murderer cannot be forgiven, as he has taken the life of one **in the image of God.** It is not a divorced person who has remarried — some will argue that such a person continually lives in adultery, but we have seen this is contrary to Scripture when I preached the message from the Sermon on the Mount series, *'The Devil Deceives the Divorced.'* The woman of Samaria, who had five husbands, would never have been saved if this were the case.

B. What is the unpardonable sin? I believe it is *a definite act (action) at a point in time when one comes to a state of soul when God gives them up.*

1. Is it simply an act of one particular sin, i.e., ascribing a miracle of Jesus to Satan, as the Pharisees did in the context of our text *(Matt. 12:24)?* Christ does not say they had committed the unpardonable sin, but their conduct seems they were well on their way to committing it.

2. Some say it is a specific utterance of blasphemy against the Holy Spirit. May I ask, why it would be more of a sin to speak blasphemy against the Holy Spirit than to speak blasphemy against the Father or the Son of the Godhead? Paul was a blasphemer, yet he was gloriously saved *(1 Tim.1:13), h*e even compelled (tried to force) believers to blaspheme *(Acts 26:11).* Paul, after he says he was a blasphemer, goes on to speak of God's exceeding abundant grace *(1 Tim. 1:14) T*he Holy Spirit is referred to as the Spirit of grace in *Heb.10:29.* I believe Paul could have committed the unpardonable sin, had he done despite, which means *to insult, to exercise violence, i.e. abuse:--use despitefully, reproach, entreat shamefully (spitefully).the Spirit of grace (30, 31).* I want you to understand it is not the rank of the person in the Godhead, for they are equal, but the increased clearness of revelation as furnished by the Spirit of grace, in the face of which a person can knowingly and willingly reject and despise—that's what aggravates the crime and makes it unpardonable.

3. I believe blasphemy against the H. G. is a state of soul to which man by repeated sinning has arrived. I believe there is a cut-off point where one can no longer receive forgiveness and can be eternally lost. It may be at the point where one sees the evidence of the Lord's power before his eyes, as the Pharisees did, and declaring it to be Satanic power; or it may be the final act of sin in continuing in homosexuality to where God gives them up; it could be continuing in other sexual sins, murder, wickedness of any kind and it could be the simple act of leaving this service and definitely putting oneself, once and for all on the side of Satan—God may never deal with you again. I also believe it can be committed by believing the false doctrine of cults who deny the deity of Christ and refusing to believe the truth *(Tit.3:9-11)*

It is a state of soul to which man by repeated sinning has arrived. **What do I mean by a** *'state of the soul'?* When I speak of the state of a man's body, you know what I mean. When I speak of the state of a man's mind, you know what I mean, but what do I mean by the state of one's soul? One's state of soul, as it relates to the things of God, is his susceptibility to the Spirit of God. I believe there are thoughts and acts of sin in which one at first may be indifferent to when the Holy Spirit deals with them, but as they resist the Spirit their resistance changes to active opposition. The Spirit may still be dealing with the individual, but his resistance and opposition may become active antagonism to the point where the soul hardens beyond the susceptibility to the Spirit of God. Therefore, I believe it can be a final act of sin where one's state of soul is beyond forgiveness—where God gives them up and it is the condition of man (his soul) rather than any action that makes his case hopeless. They reach the point of no return in their self-imposed hardness of heart. *Prov.29:1, He, that being often reproved hardeneth his neck [b*ecomes more stubborn, rebellious] *shall suddenly be destroyed, and that without remedy.* There is no mere act of sin without previous sin leading up to it *(James 1:14-16) T*he death referred to here is spiritual death, as all are subject to physical death. I believe one can reach a state of willful, determined opposition to the Holy Spirit that finally ends in that awful blasphemy —a deliberate, definite choice of rejecting God's message to their inmost being by the ministry of the Holy Ghost*--'Spirit of grace'-f*or the final time. An early theologian, Augustine, called it *'final independence.'*

I believe there are 2 marks of one who has committed the unpardonable sin: (1) opposition to spiritual things; (2) unmoved by the preaching of the Word. *Preacher, do you mean that God would no longer forgive such a person?* Whether forgiveness would be denied, if sought, is a useless question, since the sin is unpardonable, not on God's account, on account of the sinner. He virtually commits moral suicide, having forever killed his conscience and destroyed his spiritual susceptibility and removed himself from ever asking forgiveness. Repentance is a gift of God and the unpardonable sinner has driven from him the only person, the Holy Spirit, Who could ever work repentance in his heart. As Esau sold his birthright, so can one who continues to reject God to the point of being a reprobate or apostate *(Heb.12:12-17).* Esau sold his birthright, as an apostate does.

4. Some have asked if committing suicide is an unpardonable sin. There are those young people, and adults as well, who are led by the devil in the friends they chose, in the music they listen to, the movies they watch, and the drugs and the alcohol they use, leading them to a state of suicide. Obviously if one who is unsaved takes their life and instantly dies they cannot call upon God to pardon them—it is unpardonable in that sense. There have been those who from all indications were believers in Christ, and because of their depression and the medication they were on have taken their lives. Fortunately I have never had to preach the funeral of one who took their own life and I am not anxious to do so. I have preached the funeral of one who was murdered.

III. The final question is, who can commit it? The answer to that question is important, because I believe all of us are capable of committing this sin.

A.   If you are here unsaved the Bible teaches that you can become a reprobate. What is a reprobate? **(Jer.6:27-30; Rom.1:26-28** [homosexuals can be saved] **1 Cor. 6:9c, 11.** A religious person, though sincere, who has never been saved and blinded to the truth is a reprobate

B.   If you are saved, but living in rebellion against God, you too may commit the unpardonable sin and become an apostate.

C.   What is an apostate? The word is a transliteration of the Greek word 'apostasia', which is translated *'forsake'* in *Acts 21:21*and *'falling away'* in *2*

Thes.2:3. There are several warnings in Scripture that we who are saved can go back in sin, then continue in sin by willful, voluntary and intelligent turning from and rejection of God's counsel and leadership. There is a point where one who has been saved, can fall beyond repentance ***(Heb.6:4-9 [4a,.. 6a]).*** The argument of those who do not believe in apostasy is that this passage is not speaking of a saved person, but there are 5 characteristics of a saved person given: (a) ***once enlightened-t***o light, give light to, illuminate-***(10:32);*** (b) ***tasted of the heavenly gift-t***o taste, to partake of-***2:9*** ***(c) partakers of the H. G.-s***hare or participate in-***3:1, 14*** (d) ***tasted of the good word of God (***see above); (e) ***tasted of the powers of the world to come (Eph. 2:5,6)***

Christian, is there unforgiven sin in your life? Are you not where you should be with the Lord? Apostasy is God's warning for the apathetic and presumptuous. He warns of its possibility. Sin's danger is not that sin severs one's relationship with God, but that unforgiven sin hardens one's heart leading to an evil heart of unbelief in departing from the living God ***(Heb.3:12-14)***

The unpardonable sin, when may it happen? Listen to this poem, *'The Unseen Line' i*n closing and examine your relationship with God:

There is a time we know not when, a place we know not where;
That marks the destiny of man, for glory or despair.
There is a time by us unseen that crosses every path;

The hidden boundary between God's patience and His wrath.

To pass that limit is to die, to die as if by stealth;

It does not quench the beaming eye, or pale the glow of health.

The conscience may still be at ease, the spirits light and gay;

That which is pleasing, still may please, and care be thrust away.

But on the forehead God has set indelibly a mark—

Unseen by man, as yet is blind and in the dark.

And still the doomed man's path below may bloom as Eden bloomed—

He did not, does not, will not know, or feel that he is doomed.

He knows, he feels that all is well and every fear is calmed;

He lives, he dies, he wakes in hell, not only doomed but damned.

Oh, where is this mysterious bourne by which our path is crossed;

Beyond which God Himself hath sworn, that he who goes is lost.

How far may men go on in sin? How long will God forbear?

Where does hope end and where begin the confines of despair?

An answer from the skies is sent; ye that from God depart,

While it is called today, repent, and harden not your heart.

Paul tells us in *2 Cor 13:5, Examine yourselves, whether ye be in the faith; prove your own selves. Know ye not your own selves, how that Jesus Christ is in you, except ye be reprobates?*

In the introduction of the message I said that I preach on the unpardonable sin because **it is a solemn warning to all who will continue to live in sin.** Many will be living when Christ comes again who've heard the truth of Gospel and *'because they received not the love of the truth, that they might be saved, and for this cause God shall send them strong delusion, that they should believe a lie.' T*he false hope of those who will be *'left behind'* after the rapture of believers to repent and receive Jesus as Savior is clearly given in Scripture. When God says, *that they should believe a lie,* believe you me, they will believe the lies of Satan, the antichrist, if God said so and consequently they have committed the unpardonable sin. A clear warning is given that after *the wicked one* [antichrist] *is revealed, even him, whose coming is after the working of Satan with all power and signs and lying wonders, and with all deceivableness of unrighteousness in them that perish; because they received not the love of the truth, that they might be saved. And for this cause God shall send them strong delusion, that they should believe a lie: that they all might be damned who believed not the truth, but had pleasure in unrighteousness, 2 Th 2:8-12.*

I close the message with a verse I used earlier--*Heb 10:31, It is a fearful thing to fall into the hands of the living God.*

This is one of the messages of the 37 messages from the 'The Messages from 1st John,' series available on the 'Monitor Messages' CD.

The Danger of Willful Sin
Heb.10:26-31

²⁶ *For if we sin wilfully after that we have received the knowledge of the truth, there remaineth no more sacrifice for sins,*
²⁷ *But a certain fearful looking for of judgment and fiery indignation, which shall devour the adversaries.*
²⁸ *He that despised Moses' law died without mercy under two or three witnesses:*
²⁹ *Of how much sorer punishment, suppose ye, shall he be thought worthy, who hath trodden under foot the Son of God, and hath counted the blood of the covenant, wherewith he was sanctified, an unholy thing, and hath done despite unto the Spirit of grace?*
³⁰ *For we know him that hath said, Vengeance belongeth unto me, I will recompense, saith the Lord. And again, The Lord shall judge his people.*
³¹ *It is a fearful thing to fall into the hands of the living God.*

Each warning given in **Hebrews** is progressively worse. As we've seen there is the *danger of drifting away* from the truth spoken by the Son; the *danger of our doubting* the Word of God, or *unbelief,* not entering into His rest; and the danger of not going on to maturity and *committing apostasy.*

All of these are dangers for the child of God, not for the unsaved. The danger of the unsaved is not to be saved and thus go to hell—the lake of fire. *Hebrews* is to those of Israel who are believers. He is writing to us who are believers, having accepted the Lord Jesus Christ and His sacrifice for their sins. What was their problem? They, like us, needed to patiently endure. They needed to hold fast. *Heb 10:23, Let us hold fast the profession of our faith without wavering; for he is faithful that promise.* The key words in *Hebrews* is *'patience'* or *'patient endurance'* —to persevere. So after reprimanding them for not being teachers of the Word even though they had been saved long enough to be teaching, and still needing to be taught the milk, he urges them to *'go on to perfection' (6:1)*—on to maturity. The reason for doing this is because it is impossible for anyone who is saved *'if they shall fall away, to renew them again unto repentance' (6:6).* No one can be saved but once. We are only *'once saved.'* This is why there is the need to go on and a warning against going back. I closed the previous message with *Heb.6:7,8* that fits perfectly. I want to receive *'the blessing from God',* rather than *'cursing; whose end is to be burned'* don't you? I closed on the positive note found in *v.9, But, beloved, we are persuaded better things of you, and things that accompany salvation, though we thus speak.* As I've said in previous messages, we as Free Will Baptists believe as our Treatise states: *'There are strong grounds to hope that the truly regenerate will persevere unto the end, and be saved, through the power of divine grace which is pledged to their support.'*

In the previous message on the *warning of unbelief* I said, it tells us what we are to do when we discover it in the church *'exhort one another' (3:13).* We are not to condemn nor condone. We are to exhort one another by love and good works--*Heb 10:24, And let us consider one another to provoke* [stimulate] *unto love and to good works.* That is why we ought to be faithful in church attendance in these last days, as is stated in the verse previous to the text for this message *(Heb.10:25)* Why is this important? *Lest any of you be hardened through the deceitfulness of sin (3:13b), a*nd that we will not *'sin willfully.'* Today's text is *Heb.10:26-31.*

I. Who is this *warning of willful sin* addressed to? As have already said, He is writing to us who are believers, having accepted the Lord Jesus Christ and His sacrifice for our sins. In the previous message I shared the 5 characteristics of a true believer. The people he writes *Hebrews t*o be enlightened, knowledgeable, Spirit-filled, involved in Bible study, and had experienced miracles. There is a clear indication of who he is addressing in *Heb.10:26-31.* Note he says in *v.26 'we' He* includes himself along with them. *We have received the knowledge of the truth.*

Only a believer can **received the knowledge of the truth** for the natural man cannot even know the spiritual things of the Word. **But the natural man receiveth not the things of the Spirit of God: for they are foolishness unto him: neither can he know them, because they are spiritually discerned, 1 Cor 2:14; There remaineth no more sacrifice for sins,** shows that they were saved or else the sacrifice of Christ could not avail for them. The illustration of **v.29** shows they were saved, for those with Moses were blood-redeemed people and under the blood of the covenant of the law. **The blood of the covenant, wherewith they were sanctified.** The blood is applied to believers when they are saved, and as they continue walking in the light-**1 John 1:7, But if we walk in the light, as he is in the light, we have fellowship one with another, and the blood of Jesus Christ his Son cleanseth us from all sin.** We are under the blood of the covenant, and out from under wrath. No unbeliever is under the blood, nor set apart (**sanctified**) by the blood. **'The Spirit of grace'** shows they are believers. The Holy Spirit is longsuffering with unbelievers but grace is received through the Holy Spirit only with believers. We are saved by grace through faith. Grace is available to unbelievers, but we who are believers have been recipients of it. Only a believer can, then, **'do despite unto the Spirit of grace.'** The grace of the Spirit of grace is the thing involved here. The word **'despite'** has the idea in it of arrogance and willful injury, and it would involve the refusal by the believer to heed the Spirit's conviction to not commit **willful sin.** To go ahead and sin after the gracious conviction of the Spirit would be a slap to Him, and He would be grieved. A warning is given—*And grieve not the holy Spirit of God, whereby ye are sealed unto the day of redemption, Eph 4:30.* Finally, the use of the quotation from *Deu 32:36* in *v.30, 'The Lord shall judge his people,'* shows that this is a reference to believers. Judgment here is not on the world, or unbelievers, but on God's own people who are His children.

II. What does it mean to *sin willfully?* It is present tense and may be translated *'if we keep on sinning willfully after that we have received full knowledge of the truth, there remaineth no more sacrifice for sins.'* This sin is, then, a deliberate, premeditated sinning with full knowledge that it is wrong. It is a voluntary sin which the believer wills to commit after he has been saved and come to full knowledge of the truth. Now every time a believer sins it is because he *'willed'* to sin. He did not have to sin, and Paul deals with those sins in *Rom.6-8.* This act here, however, is something different. The word **'willfully'** is hekousios, means *'voluntarily, deliberately.* So we see there are two qualifications to **'willful sin':** deliberate and continuous. It is like the presumptuous sin in *Num 15:30, 31, But the soul that doeth ought presumptuously, whether he be born in the land, or a stranger, the same reproacheth the Lord; and that soul shall be cut off from among his people. Because he hath despised the word of the Lord, and hath broken his commandment, that soul shall utterly be cut off; his iniquity shall be upon him.*

If you don't see a difference in the life of one who says they are a Christian, then they are living in the danger that is given of willful sin, where **'there remaineth no** *more sacrifice for sins,* or perhaps they have never really been saved, as it tells us in *1 John 3:6, Whosoever abideth in him sinneth not: whosoever sinneth hath not seen him, neither known him.* There are continuous verbs in this verse as well, it is saying, *Whosoever abideth* [is abiding] *in him sinneth not* [does not practice sin]: *whosoever sinneth* [practices sinning] *hath not seen him, neither known him.*

Heb.10:26-31 is referring to a sustained defiance towards God--apostasy--as it was in *6:4-6,* that is for them to turn deliberately away from faith in Christ and return to their former Judaism, as if Jesus were not the Messiah at all. And so can believers identified by the 5 characteristics of Christians. Willful sin is not the kind of sins Paul deals with in *Rom.6-8,* but is flagrant, deliberate apostasy.

III. What is the nature of willful sin? It says in *1 John 1:8, If we say that we have no sin, we deceive ourselves, and the truth is not in us.* But *willful sin* is deliberate, defiant sin and is compared to *'despising* [rejecting] *the law of Moses', (v.28)* and they *'died without mercy',* that is, there was no provision for pardon. There was mercy for the ignorant, the mistaken, those *'overtaken',* but not for the deliberate despiser. Under grace there are those sins that *'overtake'* us when we fail to obey and follow the Lord, so we must not judge one of the *willful sin* our text deals with, for it tells us in *Gal 6:1, Brethren, if a man be overtaken in a fault, ye which are spiritual, restore such an one in the spirit of meekness; considering thyself, lest thou also be tempted.*

There is *'much sorer punishment'* for those who willfully sin under grace *'who hath trodden under foot the Son of God.'* Figuratively it means, *'to look upon with scorn, treat with disdain'.* Barnes says, *This language is taken either from the custom of ancient conquerors who were accustomed to tread on the necks of their enemies in token of their being subdued, or from the fact that men tread on that which they despise and contemn. The idea is, that he who should apostatize from the Christian faith would act as if he should indignantly and contemptuously trample on God's only Son. What crime could be more aggravated than this?*

A real offense of God's mercy is to *'count the blood of the covenant, wherewith we are sanctified, an unholy thing.'* The *'blood of the covenant'* means the sacrificial death of Christ, by which the new covenant between God and man was ratified, sealed, and confirmed. And counting this unholy, or common, intimates that they expected nothing from it in a sacrificial or atoning way. Jesus tells us the *'new covenant'* is ratified, or sealed and sanctioned by His blood. He tells of our blood covenant--*Mat 26:27,28, And he took the cup, and gave thanks, and gave it to them, saying, Drink ye all of it; for this is my blood of the new testament* [covenant], *which is shed for many for the remission of sins.* He says the covenant which God is about to form with men, the new covenant, is sealed or ratified with his blood, *'which is shed for many for the remission of sins'. Rom 6:23, For the wages of sin is death. Christ died for our sins according to the Scriptures, 1 Cor 15:3.* In order that sin may be forgiven, this is the way by which God will pardon transgressions. His blood is effectual for the pardon of sin because it is the life of Jesus; the blood being used as representing life itself, or as containing the elements of life.

Another character of *'willful sin'* and *'there remaineth no more sacrifice for sins,'* is when one *'hath done despite unto the Spirit of grace.'* Apostasy is when one sins away their day of grace and cannot be forgiven and it says in *Mt 12:31 Wherefore I say unto you, All manner of sin and blasphemy shall be forgiven unto men: but the blasphemy against the Holy Ghost shall not be forgiven unto men.* There is a close relation between the words *'blasphemy'* and *'despite'*: *'blasphemy'* is vilification (defamation especially against God), evil speaking, railing and *'despite'* is to exercise violence, i.e. abuse:--use despitefully, reproach, entreat shamefully (spitefully). (Strongs)

We established in the previous message—*'it is impossible for those* who believe—*if they shall fall away, to renew them again unto repentance.*

IV. The judgment of one who *willfully sins*. To such an apostate person as in *v.29* God's terrible vengeance and judgment is sure to come. *'It is a fearful thing to fall into the hands of the living God,' Heb 10:31.* Why is it *'fearful'* [dreadful]? Because God is **the living God.** He cannot be trifled with! When it says, ***there remaineth no more sacrifice for sins,*** it *says what it means and means what it says!*

We are saved by grace, but grace doesn't mean that we

can do any-thing we want. Is it possible for a believer today to be guilty of willful sin? It most certainly is, as we have seen in the previous messages. We are saved by the life-blood of Christ and the eternal guilt of sin is removed forever but it is possible to neglect this so great salvation and to carelessly *drift away* from it through indifference. It is possible to live a life of doubt and unbelief. It is possible to never mature in the Lord and never grow up, but to be infants in spiritual things all of our lives, and fall away. It is also possible to sin willfully or deliberately with full understanding of the sin and the consequences of our action, and experience the hand of God's judgment, and be lost for eternity.

The message has primarily been a warning to believers about the possibility of apostasy and not being able to repent. It is also possible for unbelievers to sin away their day of grace and become a reprobate. I said earlier, the danger of the unsaved is not to be saved and go to hell. The Bible says a reprobate is a sinner who crosses the line of no repentance. We find a reprobate 4 times in the Bible: *Jer 6:30, Reprobate silver shall men call them, because the Lord hath rejected them.* Then it speaks of those who continue to live in a homosexual lifestyle in *Rom 1: 28, And even as they did not like to retain God in their knowledge, God gave them over to a reprobate mind, to do those things which are not convenient.* The reason I said, who continue this lifestyle, for we see in *1 Cor 6:9-11* it speaks of this sin and says, *such were some of you: but ye are washed, but ye are sanctified, but ye are justified in the name of the Lord Jesus, and by the Spirit of our God.* Then it speaks of those in the last days *'ever learning, and never able to come to the knowledge of the truth', 2 Tim 3:7,* comparing them to those who withstood Moses, *so do these also resist the truth: men of corrupt minds, reprobate concerning the faith, v.8.* One more reference is found for reprobate--*Titus 1:16, They profess that they know God; but in works they deny him, being abominable, and disobedient, and unto every good work reprobate.*

Whether you have accepted Christ as Savior and not living your life as you know you should, or if you have never received Christ as Savior, I want you to listen to what it says in *2 Pet 3:9, The Lord is not slack concerning his promise, as some men count slackness; but is longsuffering to us-ward, not willing that any should perish, but that all should come to repentance.* My prayer is that you will not cross the *'unseen line'* and be forever lost as the following poem illustrates:

"There is a time we know not when, a place we know not where;
That marks the destiny of man, for glory or despair.
There is a time by us unseen that crosses every path;
The hidden boundary between God's patience and His wrath,
To pass that limit is to die, to die as if by stealth;
It does not quench the beaming eye, or pale the glow of health.
The conscience may still be at ease, the spirits light and gay;

That which is pleasing, still may please, and care be thrust away.

But on the forehead God has set indelibly a mark-
Unseen by man, as yet is blind and in the dark.
And still the doomed man's path below may bloom as Eden bloomed-
He did not, does not, will not know, or feel that he is doomed.
He knows, he feels that all is well and every fear is calmed:
He lives, he dies, he wakes in hell, not only doomed but damned.
Oh, where is this mysterious bourne by which our path is crossed;
Beyond which God Himself hath sworn, that he who goes is lost.
How far may men go on in sin? How long will God forbear?
Where does hope end and where begin the confines of despair?

An answer from the skies is sent; Ye that from God depart,
While it is called today, repent, and harden not your heart."

Christian, remember I said, the key words in *Hebrews* is *'patience'* or *'patient endurance'* —to persevere. I hope these messages of warning have been an encouragement for you to **hold fast the profession of your faith.** I close on this positive note: **Heb 10:39, But we are not of them who draw back unto perdition; but of them that believe to the saving of the soul.** We are told that 90 % of active Christians were saved before age 20; when past 25 man's odds of being saved is 5000 to 1; past 35 its

25,000 to 1; past 45 its 80,000 to 1; past 50 its 150,000 to 1. Sinner, every day you live your chances of being saved are being diminished, will you commit the unpardonable sin and spend an eternity in hell? The choice is yours!

This is one of the messages of the 6 messages from the 'Warnings in Hebrews,' series available on the 'Monitor Messages' CD.

The State of the Ship
Ezek 27:26

26 Thy rowers have brought thee into great waters: the east wind hath broken thee in the midst of the seas.

Ezek 27:26, Thy rowers have brought thee into great waters: the east wind hath broken thee in the midst of the seas. I preached concerning *The State of the Union* in January, which was quite different than the President's speech. I also dealt with the state of the church as it exists in the Union. I am an American through and through; there's no other place I want to move to; but we better wake up in America before it's too late! What I see on the horizon, unless revival comes, are some stormy waters and an east wind of God's judgment! We need to realize that the rowers have rowed us into troubled waters. This message is not politically correct, nor religiously correct [I think you know what I mean by religious]; but I do want it to be Biblically correct!

Ezek. uses a parable of a great ship to describe Tyre's condition; a ship comparable to the Titanic--**vv.4-7 Thy borders are in the midst of the seas, thy builders have perfected thy beauty. They have made all thy ship boards of fir trees of Senir: they have taken cedars from Lebanon to make masts for thee. Of the oaks of Bashan have they made thine oars; the company of the Ashurites have made thy benches of ivory, brought out of the isles of Chittim. Fine linen with broidered work from Egypt was that which thou spreadest forth to be thy sail; blue and purple from the isles of Elishah was that which covered thee.** But listen again to **Ezek 27:26, Thy rowers have brought thee into great waters: the east wind hath broken thee in the midst of the seas.** The word **"great"** means "troubled or tempestuous waters." The context of the verse indicates a great storm. The **"east wind"** was the most violent wind in the Mediterranean, and in the **"midst of the sea"** means the ship was far from shore or a haven to dock in. Reminds me of a song 'You Are Drifting Too Far From the Shore'-- we've drifted far from where we once were as a country and as a church, but as we have drifted there have been those rowers the devil has used to get us farther and farther away from our mooring to the Word of God. I'm preaching on "The State of the Ship" and some rowers who have got us where we at today.

I. Our text is dealing with the city of Tyre [Tyrus], located ½ mile from the Med.Shore, with the rest of the great city being built on the main land. The island was the most corrupt part of the city at that time, comparable to the sin and corruption in America. Through her harbors (both north/south) she was able to handle the exotic merchandise from Syria, Mesopotamia and the East. She was a proud city and felt her position in the sea left her impregnable. We're told in *chps.26-28* how the city was going to fall and God tells us why they were in the situation they were in--*Thy rowers have brought thee into great waters: the east wind hath broken thee in the midst of the seas.* Ezekiel prophecies her fate in *Ezek 26:3-7 Therefore thus saith the Lord GOD; Behold, I am against thee, O Tyrus, and will cause many nations to come up against thee, as the sea causeth his waves to come up. And they shall destroy the walls of Tyrus, and break down her towers: I will also scrape her dust from her, and make her like the top of a rock. It shall be a place for the spreading of nets in the midst of the sea: for I have spoken it, saith the Lord GOD: and it shall become a spoil to the nations. And her daughters which are in the field shall be slain by the sword; and they shall know that I am the LORD. For thus saith the Lord GOD; Behold, I will bring upon Tyrus Nebuchadnezzar king of Babylon, a king of kings, from the north, with horses, and with chariots, and with horsemen, and companies, and much people.* Nebuchadnezzar did attack Tyre, took the main land and laid siege on the island for 13 years, but was not able to take the island city.

Some critics probably said Ezekiel's prophecy was wrong and not from God. But when God says something, we can rest assured it will happen; 250 years later (333 BC) Alexander the Great made his way down the Mediterranean Coast and eliminated Tyre, which was potentially dangerous to his supply lines. He literally scraped the main land of Tyre into the harbor to build a causeway to the island so he could destroy it--***26:4b, I will also scrape her dust from her, and make her like the top of a rock.*** Today one can stand on the bare rocky foundation of this once great city and watch the fisherman laying their nets out to dry--***26:5a It shall be a place for the spreading of nets in the midst of the sea: for I have spoken it, saith the Lord GOD.*** What a vivid example of the truthfulness of God's Word and the literalness of its fulfillment.

Humanism didn't begin with John Dewey in the public school system, it has been around since Adam and Eve. The king of Tyre tried to humanize God and deify man; he attributed to himself superhuman wisdom; a wisdom that achieved for him wealth and power. God sent Ezekiel to tell him that he was man and not God-- ***Ezek 28:1-10, The word of the LORD came again unto me, saying, Son of man, say unto the prince of Tyrus, Thus saith the Lord GOD; Because thine heart is lifted up, and thou hast said, I am a God, I sit in the seat of God, in the midst of the seas; yet thou art a man, and not God, though thou set thine heart as the heart of God: Behold, thou art wiser than Daniel; there is no secret that they can hide from thee: With thy wisdom and with thine understanding thou hast gotten thee riches, and hast gotten gold and silver into thy treasures: By thy great wisdom and by thy traffic hast thou increased thy riches, and thine heart is lifted up because of thy riches: Therefore thus saith the Lord GOD; Because thou hast set thine heart as the heart of God; Behold, therefore I will bring strangers upon thee, the terrible of the nations: and they shall draw*** *their swords against the beauty of thy wisdom, and they shall defile thy brightness. They shall bring thee down to the pit, and thou shalt die the deaths of them that are slain in the midst of the seas. Wilt thou yet say before him that slayeth thee, I am God? but thou shalt be a man, and no God, in the hand of him that slayeth thee. Thou shalt die the deaths of the uncircumcised by the hand of strangers: for I have spoken it, saith the Lord GOD.*

The thing that proved he was not God was his death. We see who the real king of Tyre is, as God pulls back the veil to allow us to see the power that energized the king of Tyre and in *vv.11-19* we see some words which do not speak of a man, but speaks of Lucifer as he is named in *Isa.14:12. Ezek 28:13 Thou hast been in Eden the garden of God; v.14 Thou art the anointed cherub that covereth; and I have set thee so: thou wast upon the holy mountain of God; v.15 Thou wast perfect in thy ways from the day that thou wast created, till iniquity was found in thee.* Our enemy is not flesh and blood--*Eph.6:12, For we wrestle not against flesh and blood, but against principalities, against powers, against the rulers of the darkness of this world, against spiritual wickedness in high places.* Lucifer's great sin was pride; this is what caused his fall-*Ezek 28:17 Thine heart was lifted up because of thy beauty, thou hast corrupted thy wisdom by reason of thy brightness: I will cast thee to the ground, I will lay thee before kings, that they may behold thee.* Satan continues to use the destructive weapon of pride on all who will yield to him; he knows pride will keep anyone away from the Lord—his favorite tool. Too many preachers are worried more about a reputation than repentance.

Ezek. describes Tyre as a ship and the people on the ship being moved into a tempestuous storm; the east wind is about to destroy them. Some were not aware of who was rowing them into being *"broken in the midst of the seas".*

II. How does this all apply to America? I believe you've already seen how it applies. Our nation in the past was a Christian nation; God has blessed us because in the past we followed the precepts of the Word. But our past righteousness will not withhold the judgment of God, whether it be a nation or individuals--*Ezek 33:13 When I shall say to the righteous, that he shall surely live; if he trust to his own righteousness, and commit iniquity, all his righteousnesses shall not be remembered; but for his iniquity that he hath committed, he shall die for it. Prov 14:34 Righteousness exalteth a nation: but sin is a reproach to any people.* We like Tyre are in some troubled waters!

What Happened-Retired Navy Chaplain

Let's see. . I think it started when Madalyn Murray O'Hair complained that she didn't want any prayer in our schools, and we said OK. Then someone said, you better not read the Bible in school--for it says thou shalt not kill, thou shalt not steal, and love thy neighbor as thyself. And we said OK.

Dr. Benjamin Spock said that we shouldn't spank our children when they misbehave because their little personalities would be warped and we might damage their self-esteem. And we said an expert should know what he is talking about, so we won't spank them anymore. Then someone said that teachers and principals better not discipline our children when they misbehave and school administrators said, no faculty member in this school better touch a child when they misbehave because we don't want any bad publicity, and we surely don't want to be sued. We accepted their reasoning.

Then someone said, let's let our daughters have abortions if they want, and they won't even have to tell their parents. And we said, that's a grand idea.

Then some school board member said, since boys will be boys and they are going to "do it" anyway, let's give our sons all the contraceptives they want, so they can have all the "fun" they desire, and we won't have to tell their parents they got them at school and we said, that's another great idea.

And then some of our top elected officials said it doesn't matter what we do in private as long as we do our jobs. Agreeing with them, we said it does not matter to me what anyone, including the President, does in private as long as I have a job and the economy is good.

And then someone said, let's promote sexual exploitation of women in print and on the internet, and call it art. And we said they're entitled to their free speech. And someone else took that appreciation a step further and said let's promote sexual exploitation of children and use the powerful homosexual lobby to legitimize such abuse. And we said we must be tolerant of diversity.

And the entertainment industry said, let's make TV shows and movies that promote the most evil attributes of our humanity. Let's record music that encourages rape, drugs, murder, suicide, and satanic themes. and we said, give us more.

Now we are asking ourselves who so many of our nation's youth have no conscience, why they don't know right from wrong, and why it doesn't bother them to kill strangers, their classmates, and themselves. What happened? If we contemplate this question vigorously, we might determine the answer!"

Who are the rowers who have rowed us into troubled waters, while America sits idly on the deck not realizing what has happened to us? You already know what I'm about to tell you—liberals have rowed us to where we are:

A. Liberal politicians. Conservatives have a problem in Washington, as they must barter and bargain with liberals—*"we'll vote for this, if you will vote for that"* ; the next thing you know they have ahold of the oars rowing us into deeper water. Some who once voted against the desecration of the flag, no longer vote what the people they represent want. Some won't even vote for the 10 Commandments to be displayed in public schools [they need displayed in the Oval office]; someone said if they did vote for their display there the President would line item veto a couple of them. I was handing out the booklet, *"It's Time to Reclaim Our Nation--Enough is Enough"* and went to this one door. I usually do not agree with a drunk; I usually do not agree with a Catholic; but I did agree with a drunk Catholic who said our President has got our country in a mess.

B. Liberal judges have helped row us to where we are. Even on the local level; police officers risk their lives to apprehend the criminal, then some liberal judge will let them back out on the street. The liberal Supreme Court Judges made a decision and now we've killed over 37M unborn babies(over 5 times as many Jews as Hitler killed). The people who murder their babies go on in their free love lifestyle; then there's the liberal courts/politician's view on the perverts [queers, sodomites]. I believe AIDS is the whirlwind of God's end-time judgment on the sodomites and drug heads as it tells us in *Jer.30:23,24, Behold, the whirlwind of the LORD goeth forth with fury, a continuing whirlwind: it shall fall [remain] with pain upon the head of the wicked. The fierce anger of the LORD shall not return, until he have done it, and until he have performed the intents of his heart: in the latter days ye shall consider it.* You talk us about being rowed into troubled waters; we've only seen the tip of the iceberg of this plague of AIDS on our society. I have a set of videos, *"You Just Think You're Safe,"* which relates how easy AIDS is spread. *God has a cure for AIDS!* It's the Gospel message that will change the lifestyle of these people, if they will believe the Gospel and repent of their sins.

C. The liberal media has helped row us into troubled waters. They only report what they want you to hear, while they report and promote the liberal views of our politicians and the courts. <u>They are the ones who</u> champion the rights of the baby killers and sodomites . . are not telling the whole truth about AIDS . . condition our minds and get us to listen, see, and read what they want us to, and many are unknowingly being rowed into troubled waters. The business of the entertainment media is to amuse us [muse means to think, "a" negates it]. Fools make a mock of sin-that's why the situation comedies get people laughing at drunkenness. .adultery. .homosexuals and perverts--they mock sin. ***Prov 14:9 Fools make a mock at sin.*** Many believers allow those on TV to do and say things in their living room they wouldn't think of allowing a few years ago. Many now laugh at what they used to hate. I preach a message-*"What Are You Laughing At?"-n*ot too popular with some!

D. Liberal theologians in our colleges and "cemeteries"[seminaries] and the **liberal preachers** have helped to row us into troubled waters. We have many congregations who walk, talk, act and smell like the world as a result of some preachers not preaching separation from the world. We have those who preach a gray area of sin rather than darkness and light, but I sure don't want the woe of the Lord to be on my preaching, as it is with theirs—***Isa.5: 20,21 Woe unto them that call evil good, and good evil; that put darkness for light, and light for darkness; that put bitter for sweet, and sweet for bitter! Woe unto them that are wise in their own eyes, and prudent in their own sight!.*** We have come to the place where some in the church can no longer define what is worldly; they cannot tell the difference between the holy and the profane; they don't have their senses exercised to discern both good and evil, **cf. Heb 5:14.** Entertainment in the church is accepted by many as worship to a holy God, preachers would rather give the people what they want rather than what they need--when the Bible is no longer considered the final authority. Some promote Promise Keepers, the ecumenical men's movement that promotes *"unity in diversity."* Some of us preach dress standards that are modest for our youth, then we have youth directors, preachers/preacher's wives publicly wearing shorts, or wearing tights that reveal every freckle, like one preacher's wife at our youth camp. Many youth camps no longer have any standards and we need to tell them about it. The pulpits in FWB churches are not what they were when I was growing up; my dad had an 8th grade education, but had common enough sense to preach what the KJV Bible said and not some new perversion, like some are preaching from today. He preached what it said, not what some professor or commentary said. There was a compliment paid to him and my Uncle Ray Tallent, an old time Methodist preacher, in an anniversary booklet printed at Union Light Church (a church which is Free Will Baptist and Congregational Methodist). The person wrote that when John Long and Ray Tallent preached you felt like you were going to hell, even though you knew better. We better get back to hellfire and brimstone preaching in our pulpits, and preaching separation and some Biblical standards if we expect to reach this generation for Christ!

E. Liberal, humanistic public education has rowed us into troubled waters. Is it any wonder that we have kids killing kids--teens have the highest suicide rate--they are told by evolutionist teaching they are no more than an animal—that's why many are acting like animals, as they've been taught the survival of the fittest. What has happened in our public schools? Prayer is out/policemen are in; Bibles are out/values clarification is in; Ten Commandments are out/murder, rape, robbery, gang warfare, cheating is in. The teaching that we're created in the image and likeness of God is out/evolution is in; corporal punishment is out/disrespect and rebellion are in; traditional values are out/unwed mothers are in; abstinence is out/ free contraceptives are in and abortion is in; learning is out/social engineering is in; history is out /revisionism is in. A lot more could be said about schools.

G. Liberal parents of our day are helping row us into troubled waters that will bring the east wind of God's judgment, unless we see revival in the homes of America. We have a bunch of parents who are still acting like teenagers' who have no restraint; consequently they don't have any restraints on their children. There are many children who are going to be shipwrecked, or already shipwrecked, because of the arrogance, pride and greed of parents, who are not doing what they ought to do in guiding their children into a safe and secure haven. They make shipwreck of their own life and faith, while their children are bound to the mast of their ship of ignorance!

This is not from some fundamentalist preacher, but it's from *U.S. News and World Report:* *"100,000 of America's children are in prison; 65 of every 1000 children between the ages of 7-11 have already received psychiatric help. 1M girls between the ages of 12-17 will get pregnant this year and have a child, that's not counting those who will have an abortion; 1 in 5 of America's children use drugs twice a week. 10M American children are infected with some kind of venereal disease; the suicide rate among children is staggering —between 10-15% of America's children have tried or seriously contemplated it--some as young as 6-7 years old; every 22 minutes someone dies as a result of an alcohol related car accident and most likely beer is involved and the odds are 1 in 3 they are 15-24 years old."*

Teenagers now tell their parents where they are going rather than asking permission to go—they go where they want to go, do what they want to do, say what they want to say, and dress the way they want to dress[undress] because that's the way their parents undress. Women used to dress like Mother Hubbard, but now they dress like her cupboard--her cupboard was bare!

III. How have we allowed our nation, churches, and homes to be rowed into troubled waters? How have we been deluded and made not to think? You may think it's a strange answer to that question, but God's blessings--prosperity has caused us to not be aware of the rowers rowing us into troubled waters! Materialism is one of the greatest plagues in America! Tyre was an industrialized city of her day--***Ezek 27:24-27, These were thy merchants in all sorts of things, in blue clothes, and broidered work, and in chests of rich***

apparel, bound with cords, and made of cedar, among thy merchandise. The ships of Tarshish did sing of thee in thy market: and thou wast replenished, and made very glorious in the midst of the seas. Thy rowers have brought thee into great waters: the east wind hath broken thee in the midst of the seas. Thy riches, and thy fairs, thy merchandise, thy mariners, and thy pilots, thy calkers, and the occupiers of thy merchandise, and all thy men of war, that are in thee, and in all thy company which is in the midst of thee, shall fall into the midst of the seas in the day of thy ruin. *"Merchant and merchandise"* used 12 times in *chp.27,* indicating the wealth and prosperity of Tyre. Does this not describe America? Were it not for our prosperity, things would be different in Washington, DC. There was a campaign slogan which said, *"It's the economy stupid!"* We can say that of the moral decay and spiritual decline we see in America--*"It's the economy stupid!"* We had better quit letting our billfolds determine how we view sin, not only in the White House, but in our house as well! We better first of all, be sure our anchor holds and grips the solid rock, and we better get busy rescuing the perishing and caring for the dying. I could close the message and say, you other preachers preach us out of these troubled waters I've preached us into, but I won't close yet.

A number of years ago a submarine sank off the coast of New England; rescue workers immediately went down to try to rescue the men trapped inside; because of electrical problems the only way they could communicate with one another was to tap out messages in Morse code on the side of the submarine. After a while, this message came from inside the submarine, *"Is there any hope?"* Today many people are looking at the condition of our country, our churches and our homes and they are asking the same question- *"Is there any hope?"*

I'm here to tell you, there is hope in this hopeless generation and that hope is Jesus Christ. Even if the east wind of God's judgment falls on America and we are broken in the midst of the sea, I have the assurance of a life boat to carry me safely to Heaven's shore. I can have peace, even in the midst of the storm. *"There is peace in the time of trouble, there is peace in the midst of the storm".* If you are here lost, your condition is described very well in **Isa 57:20,21, But the wicked are like the troubled sea, when it cannot rest, whose waters cast up mire and dirt. There is no peace, saith my God, to the wicked.** . If you are lost on the sea of sin, why don't you grab the lifeline of salvation and come aboard the "Old Ship of Zion?" and if there's any believer here not doing what you can to bring revival to our country and to our churches, I hope this message and those to follow in the conference will stir your hearts to revival! We need to be helping those who are drifting away for the Word! *Throw out the lifeline across the dark wave, there is a brother whom someone should save; somebody's brother, O who then will dare to throw out the lifeline, his peril to share. Throw out the lifeline, throw out the lifeline! Someone is drifting away. Throw out the lifeline, throw out the lifeline! Someone is sinking today!*

With every head bowed and every eye closed, in closing I share with you a verse that we all know and we better take heed to--*II Chron.7:14, If my people, which are called by my name, shall humble themselves, and pray, and seek my face, and turn from their wicked ways; then will I hear from heaven, and will forgive their sin, and will heal their land..*

Preached at the 'Help Build the Fire' Pigeon Forge Preaching Conference 8/30/99

Is There Not Here a Prophet?
I Kings 22:4-8

3 And the king of Israel said unto his servants, Know ye that Ramoth in Gilead is ours, and we be still, and take it not out of the hand of the king of Syria?

4 And he said unto Jehoshaphat, Wilt thou go with me to battle to Ramothgilead? And Jehoshaphat said to the king of Israel, I am as thou art, my people as thy people, my horses as thy horses.

5 And Jehoshaphat said unto the king of Israel, Enquire, I pray thee, at the word of the LORD to day.

6 Then the king of Israel gathered the prophets together, about four hundred men, and said unto them, Shall I go against Ramothgilead to battle, or shall I forbear? And they said, Go up; for the Lord shall deliver it into the hand of the king.

7 And Jehoshaphat said, Is there not here a prophet of the LORD besides, that we might enquire of him?

8 And the king of Israel said unto Jehoshaphat, There is yet one man, Micaiah the son of Imlah, by whom we may enquire of the LORD: but I hate him; for he doth not prophesy good concerning me, but evil. And Jehoshaphat said, Let not the king say so.

Several of us who were concerned about some things we saw happening in our Free Will Baptist denomination met together in a hotel room in Nashville back in Dec., '94. We prayed together that night seeking what the Lord would have us do to bring revival back into our churches. We came to the conclusion that we needed to start having a conference for like-minded people where we could come together for a preaching conference at least once a year. We were accused of being trouble makers by the *'Fellowship of Discouragement.'*

Remember that Elijah was accused of being a trouble maker in *1 Ki 18:17,18 And it came to pass, when Ahab saw Elijah, that Ahab said unto him, Art thou he that troubleth Israel? And he answered, I have not troubled Israel; but thou, and thy father's house, in that ye have forsaken the commandments of the Lord.* Listen to *Jer 6:16, Thus saith the Lord, Stand ye in the ways, and see, and ask for the old paths, where is the good way, and walk therein, and ye shall find rest for your souls.* Notice: *But they said, We will not walk therein.* The most important words in that verse are: *Thus saith the Lord.* Likewise the most important thing I will say tonight is what God says in His Word.

One preacher said of his being on the program with some other great speakers: '*I feel like a MO mule at the Kentucky Derby'*. We have some great preachers on the program this year, I have had 3 of the speakers in my home and in the churches I have pastored, all of them more than one time. Bro. Rick Cash and Bro. John Williams who are speaking tomorrow morning, and Dr. Joe Ange who is speaking tomorrow evening. I believe they will help build the fire that is desperately needed in our day. You have often heard when men such as these speak—*'If that don't light your fire your wood is wet!'*

I want to say concerning the theme of our conference *'Help Build the Fire,'* you cannot build a fire with wet wood! A watered down Gospel will never bring the fires of revival. *Jer 23:29, Is not my word like as a fire?* Likewise, a quenching of the Spirit, where the Word of God *is being* preached, will hinder and prevent the fires of revival! It says in *1 Th 5:19-23, Quench not the Spirit. Despise not prophesyings. Prove all things; hold fast that which is good. Abstain from all appearance of evil. And the very God of peace sanctify you wholly; and I pray God your whole spirit and soul and body be preserved blameless unto the coming of our Lord Jesus Christ.* Too many in our churches are quenching the Spirit, they are despising, which simply means they are not regarding what the preacher says from the Word of God. Instead of proving by the Bible that which is being preached and holding fast to righteous living and abstaining from the appearance of evil, they go on in the way they want to live and are not living sanctified [separated] lives.

I had studied and had every intention of preaching on *'Removing the Ancient Landmarks'* which I believe is a real problem with many preachers today, but I'm convinced the Lord directed me to preach this message Now I know who I'm preaching to tonight—I'm preaching to those of us who are preachers! I'll keep in mind that when I'm pointing one finger at you there are 3 others pointing back at me. If we really want to help build the fires of revival, then we better not water down the Gospel. We better be faithful as Jeremiah was to **'thus saith the Lord'** even though others **'will not walk therein.'** I have tried my best to be faithful in preaching God's Word and I have not changed my message as many have over the years. You can ask my family, or those who have been a vital part of my ministry.

When Bro. Roy called me and said that I would be speaking this evening, I was studying for a message on sanctification in the series on the Free Will Baptist Treatise. Then the next day I received an e-mail on *'the old paths'* in **Jer 6:16.** It is a very fitting reading on the subject of separation from the world, which is lacking in our day. Many of us who are *'older',* notice I didn't say old, can relate it: **I like the old paths....**when moms were at home; dads were at work; brothers went into the army and sisters got married <u>before h</u>aving children! Crime did not pay; hard work did; and people knew the difference. Moms could cook; dads would work; and children would behave. Husbands were loving; wives were supportive and children were polite. Women wore the jewelry and men wore the pants. Women looked like ladies, men looked like gentlemen and children looked decent. People loved the truth and hated a lie. They came to church to get <u>in, n</u>ot to get <u>out!</u> Hymns sounded Godly; sermons sounded helpful; rejoicing sounded normal and crying sounded sincere; cursing was wicked; drinking was evil; and divorce was unthinkable. The flag was honored; America was beautiful; and God was welcome! We read the Bible in public; prayed in school; and preached from house to house. To be called an American was worth dying for; to be called a Christian was worth living for; to be called a traitor was a shame! Sex was a personal word; homosexual was an unheard of word; and abortion was an illegal word. Off color jokes were only told among dirty men folk. Preachers preached because they had a message and Christians rejoiced because they had the <u>victory!</u> Preachers preached from the Bible; singers sang from the heart; and sinners turned to the Lord to be <u>saved!</u> A new birth meant a new life; salvation meant a changed life; and following Christ led to eternal life. Being a preacher meant you proclaimed the Word of God; being a deacon meant you would serve the Lord. Being a Christian meant you would live for Jesus and being a sinner meant someone was praying for you!

Laws were based on the Bible; homes read the Bible; and churches taught the Bible. Preachers were more interested in new converts than new clothes and new cars. God was worshiped; Christ was exalted; and the Holy Spirit was respected. Church was where you found Christians on the Lord's Day, rather than in the garden, on the creek bank, on the golf course, or being entertained somewhere else. **I still like the Old Paths the best! Amen!!**

I don't agree with all that George Barna reports, but I found it interesting that in February he reported in a new nationwide survey conducted by his group that indicates most adults in America remain confused, if not daunted, by the concept of holiness. I will not bore you with his statistics, but once again, the responses of born again and unsaved adults were virtually identical. I fear that these statistics are true in many Free Will Baptist churches, and part of the reason is that preachers are not preaching on holiness—separation from the world—like they once did. Bro. John and I recently attended a Leadership Institute and there was a session on *'blended worship.'* If you don't know what that is, it is blending *'contemporary'* music with traditional music, as Rick Warren promotes in his *'40 Days of Purpose'.* I spoke up and said that it sounded to me like *'The Church Walking with the World'* as graphically described in the poem. Those of you familiar with the poem knows that it starts out by saying: *The Church and the World walked far apart on the changing shore of time; The World was singing a giddy song and the Church a hymn sublime.* At the end of the poem it tells the plight of a compromising church with the world: *They of the Church, and they of the World journeyed closely, hand and heart, And none but the* Master, who knoweth all, could discern the two apart. It's a long poem and I have printed copies of it available and it is on the CD.

I mentioned earlier King Ahab's confrontation with Elijah, and four chapters later he has another confrontation with a man of God who didn't compromise. *(1 Ki 22:4-8).* My message is: *'Is There Not Here a*

Prophet?'

Ahab, King of Israel, is a man who got what he wanted. He wanted Naboth's vineyard—he got it! He and Jezebel are still paying for it in hell! He also got what he wanted in the prophets prophesying for him. He is in a joint venture with Jehosophat, king of Judah, going against their common enemy, Syria. Because of the tenacity of the prophet Micaiah, I felt lead to preach on him for my own good, if no one else's. So many in our day are like Ahab. *2 Tim 4:3, For the time will come when they will not endure sound doctrine; but after their own lusts shall they <u>heap to</u> themselves teachers, having itching ears.* 'Heap' *in* Strong's--to accumulate further, i.e. (fig.) seek additionally. Ahab heaped to himself a whole heap of prophets who tickled his ears. They said what he wanted to hear *(v.6).* A lot of people still think if you can get enough people to agree on something that it's all right, but that is not true. Bro. John Rhodes preached yesterday at our church a message which dealt with the question, *'What is our attitude toward sin?'* There is a famine of the Word in our land and some are asking as Jehosophat did *(v.7),* but as a whole, people care not to hear *'thus saith the Lord,' a*nd they could care less if it doesn't agree with their lifestyle. Many will say they believe the Bible to be literally true, and it is to be literally interpreted, until it speaks against something they are doing, or want to do. Then they quit literally interpreting it-*'The Bible doesn't really mean that, it means this.' We* need some Micaiah's in our day and I believe we have some here this week. I sure don't have much use for a preacher, and neither should you, who'll sugar-coat messages to please the people he pastors. When I preached here before I told you about my dad who had an 8th grade education, but had common enough sense to preach what the KJV Bible said and not some new perversion, like some are preaching from today. He preached what it said, not what some professor or commentary said. There was a compliment paid to him and my Uncle Ray Tallent, an old time Methodist preacher, in an anniversary booklet printed at Union Light Church (a church which is Free Will Baptist and Congregational Methodist). The person wrote that when John Long and Ray Tallent preached you felt like you were going to hell, even though you knew better. We better get back to hellfire and brimstone preaching in our pulpits, and preaching separation and some Biblical standards if we expect to reach this generation for Christ!

Micaiah was a noble man, like Elijah was. I pray to God that I can be a man like he was. I hope our churches will want men like Micaiah was, but I know some of them don't like the kind of preaching that calls sin 'sin.' Any church that ever gets a preacher who will compromise what the Word of God says to satisfy some in the church, they had better call for a vote of the church.

I want to answer 3 things about this man of God, not just as information, but as a challenge to all of us when the question is asked, **Is there not a prophet?**

The questions are: *Who was he? How was he treated? Was he proven right?*

I. Who was he? I can't give you his family background, other than he was the son of Imlah *(v.8).* The last we hear of him is in prison, his last words being, ***Hearken, O people, every one of you, v.28.*** Those are some great last words. The Bible does tell us some things about this man of God, Micaiah:

A. He was a holy man, Ahab knew he was a man who knew the mind of the Lord *(v.8).* His name means, *'Who is like God.'* *I*n His character he was like God, in his testimony there was none like God. He was God's mouthpiece like all of us are to be, as we preach, *'thus saith the Lord'.* Ahab knew what his answer was before he asked him, and so it should be with us. One of our more liberal pastors in Nashville several years ago ask me, *'Where do you stand on the wine issue'?* My answer to him was—*'You know where I stand!'*

B. He was tempted to compromise his message *(v.13).* The one sent to get him tried to persuade him to speak words pleasing to the king, as the other prophets had done. The temptation was to please man rather then God. Paul was like Micaiah-***Gal 1:10, For do I now persuade men, or God? or do I seek to please men? for if I yet pleased men, I should not be the servant of Christ.***

The king's 400 false prophets had all ***with one mouth*** *(*one accord) spoken smooth things. The man who stands in God's stead must be prepared to stand alone. Men-pleasers always speak smooth things. I was told by an evangelist several years ago that there are some Free Will Baptist churches where the pastors warn them, *'You* *can't preach too hard on separation and standards here.'* God help us! Or should I say God help them! I've never been confronted with such a statement and I hope I never am. Those of us Free Will Baptist preachers who still interpret and preach the Bible literally, when it comes to separation and standards, as well as Free Will Baptist doctrine, would not last 2 weeks in some of our churches. That's a shame, but I know it to be true. *Is there not a prophet-- a preacher, who speaks out? Go*d help us to keep preaching *'thus saith the Lord.'* When we do this we will be out of step with the times, but praise be to God, we'll be in step with the Lord! The areas where many preachers fail to preach the Word literally concerns separated living, on how people dress, or should I say undress. I said in my previous message— Women used to dress like Mother Hubbard, but now they dress like her cupboard--her cupboard was bare! Many fail to preach on fornication and how people's habits defile their bodies. The Bible speaks clearly concerning our bodies. *It* does make a difference how people dress; and what they consume that defiles our bodies-**1 Cor 3:16,17 Know ye not that ye are the temple of God, and that the Spirit of God dwelleth in you? If any man defile the temple of God, him shall God destroy; for the temple of God is holy, which temple ye are.** That is what the Bible says literally!

C. Micaiah was faithful *(v.14).* Martin Luther stood before the Catholic hierarchy to be tried, he was told that the whole world was against him, his answer was, *'Then I am against the whole world!'* The faithful preacher will never shun to declare the whole counsel of God. Paul said, **For I have not shunned to declare unto you all the**

counsel of God, Acts 20:27. Listen to *Jer 23: 28, He that hath my word, let him speak my word faithfully.* God help us as preachers to continue to be like Micaiah in these last days we are living in. **Who was Micaiah? He was a holy, uncompromising, literal interpreting, fundamental, FWB preacher of his day. We** need more like him in our day! Support and pray for preacher's who continue to preach the Bible!

II. How was Micaiah treated? We find some parallels here to the pastor or evangelist who preaches hard against sin and holds to Biblical separation, when the majority of people will pay him no mind and go ahead and live the way they want to live. I must speak the truth-*Eph 4:15, Speaking the truth in love, ye may grow up into him in all things, which is the head, even Christ:* I am 'committed to changeless Christ in a changing world' I've never been treated like Micaiah was; I may be sometime in the future. **How was he treated?**

A. He was hated. Why did the king hate him? *(v.8b)* He hated him because he was no back-scratchier, or ear tickler; his words were not smooth enough for the royal ears of the king. The worldly crowd hates the truth. *John 15:18, If the world hate you, ye know that it hated me before it hated you.* Some of the most hated people in America are fundamental preachers who stand firm on the Word of God, who speak out on sodomy and abortion –the ungodly pro-abortion crowd and the gay-liberators vent their hatred all the time against those who oppose them.

B. He was mocked *(v.24).* What do false prophets, or

do men-pleasers of our day know about the Spirit of God? They have no place in the *'ministry.'* Zedekiah was the bird that put on a show and lied to Ahab *(v.11).* It seems he was the leader of these nearly 400 false prophets *(v.12).* One who takes a stand on the Word of God may not be physically hit like Micaiah was, but those opposing them are always ready to smite them with their tongue, which if said to the wrong person, at the wrong time, will hurt one's ministry more than if they would have been slapped them in the face. Micaiah told it like it was *(v.23).* This was more than Zedekiah, the false prophet, could take in front of the king and other prophets, so he slapped him and mocked him.

C. He was imprisoned *(26,27).* The self-seeking don't like the truth, so Ahab says, *'I'll get him out of the way.' Th*at's what a lot of churches do when the preacher comes down hard on their sin; they just vote him out, they get him out of the way. It was easy for Ahab, since he was the king, to bind the servant of God, but the Word of God cannot be bound. Paul said, **Wherein I suffer trouble, as an evil doer, even unto bonds; but the word of God is not bound, 2 Tim 2:9.** God's people, though rotting in Muslim prisons, have a freedom the world knows nothing about-**John 8:32, And ye shall know the truth, and the truth shall make you free.** It is evident that Ahab didn't have the freedom of mind that Micaiah had. He thought, just suppose the prophet I hate is right, so he went into battle fearful for his life--**1 Ki 22:30 And the king of Israel disguised himself, and went into the battle.** Once *'thus saith the Lord' is* spoken to any person concerning any sin in their life, they don't soon forget it! Why is this so? **Heb 4:12,13 For the word of**

God is quick, and powerful, and sharper than any twoedged sword, piercing even to the dividing asunder of soul and spirit, and of the joints and marrow, and is a discerner of the thoughts and intents of the heart. Neither is there any creature that is not manifest in his sight: but all things are naked and opened unto the eyes of him with whom we have to do. They tried to silence John Bunyan when they put him in prison, but one writer says, *'Pilgrim's Progress' came out of the jail and has been wandering throughout the world ever since.' He* wrote that great classic while he was in prison. *So we see how Micaiah was treated. How are you treated? Have you suffered any persecution, any ridicule for your stand for righteousness? If you haven't, just maybe you've not taken a strong stand against sin. **2 Tim 3:12 Yea, and all that will live godly in Christ Jesus shall suffer persecution. (** 1 Pet 4:16; 3:13-17)*

III. Was Micaiah proven right when he said what he did in *v.17?* The test of a true prophet was whether their prophecy was fulfilled *(Deu 18:21,22).*

A. His prophecy was fulfilled, even though Ahab failed to believe him. The king ordered him locked up and given bread and water until he return in peace. The next to the last thing we have recorded that Micaiah said- **1 Ki 22: 28 And Micaiah said, If thou return at all in peace, the LORD hath not spoken by me.** His prophecy of *v.17 wa*s fulfilled in *v.37.*

B. It was fulfilled, although the Ahab disguised himself to escape it *(v.30).* No man has ever been able to disguise himself so that God could not find him. God took a *'bow at a venture,' v.34* [shot at random] and it was the divine detective appointed by God to find Ahab, and find him it did, in a small space *'between the joints of the harness'* [the armor]. God's arrows never miss the mark! There are many ways that unbelievers or half-hearted believers, try to disguise themselves, with the hope of escaping God's judgment, or the consequences of their half-hearted living. **Num 32:23, Be sure your sin will find you out.** The cloak of morality or religion will never hide from God the sin of an unbelieving or rebellious heart **for the LORD seeth not as man seeth; for man looketh on the outward appearance, but the LORD looketh on the heart, 1 Sam 16:7** .

    C. Micaiah's prophecy was fulfilled, because it was God's word (v.14) Isa 55:11, So shall my word be that goeth forth out of my mouth: it shall not return unto me void, but it shall accomplish that which I please, and it shall prosper in the thing whereto I sent it. When God says something, whether it be prophecy, or about the way we're living our lives, we better take heed, for we must give account, not only of every idle word we speak **(Matt.12:36),** but we'll also give account for every word we hear, or read, from this Book. It says in **Heb 13:17** I'm going to give account to God to faithfully preach what this Book literally says, I'm going to continue to preach it like it is. Some may say as they did to Martin Luther, *'The whole worlds against you,'* then I must say as he did, *'Then I'm against the world!'* Micaiah's last recorded words shows his tenacity and how he didn't give up to the end—**Hearken, O people, every one of you, 1 Ki 22:28.** Preacher, what will be your last recorded words?

It tells us in *Rom 15:4 For whatsoever things were written aforetime were written for our learning, that we through patience and comfort of the scriptures might have hope.* I believe that **1 Kings 22 'aforetime'** is for us today.

I would like to see the hands of every preacher here tonight. Look around and see those whom God has called to be His messengers to help build the fires of revival. But let me tell you, if your wood is wet the fire is not going to start. If you are watering down the Word, or if you are quenching the Spirit, as He speaks to you tonight, you will hear these great men of God this week and leave this conference no better than when you came. I really believe the Lord led me to preach this message to preachers tonight; to some who need to nail it down and be like Micaiah was—holy, uncompromising, and faithful. Maybe you are facing opposition at the present time as a result of your stand on righteousness and you need to come and pray. If you are a layperson who has a Godly preacher, yet you are quenching the Spirit when He speaks the Word to you, then you need to make a decision tonight!

Preached at the 'Help Build the Fire' Pigeon Forge Preaching Conference 6/12/06

Section Two
Weights and Besetting Sins
Fact Sheets

Weights and Besetting Sins
Fact Sheet 1

What Is Wrong With Body Marking [Tattoos] And Body Piercing?

1. What does the Bible say about it?
The current popularity of tattoos and body piercing makes it a valid issue demanding a Christian, Biblical response. When dealing with controversial issues, many want chapter and verse in the Bible that deals namely and specifically with that issue. Those who do so fail to realize the nature of the Bible. The Bible is a book of principles that apply to any age, any culture, any person, any matter of life and living. Suppose the Bible specifically addressed every item, issue, and idea of every age, culture, and person. One would need a semi-truck to bring his Bible to church. The reason the Bible is applicable to every age and every person and every culture, is that, even if it doesn't address an issue specifically, it deals with it by its principles. There is also what is called the tenor of Scripture. The tenor of Scripture is its very nature--all that it conveys, stands for, means.

First, let's look at what has been used as chapter and verse in reference to tattoos and body piercing: *Lev 19:28 Ye shall not make any cuttings in your flesh for the dead, nor print any marks upon you: I am the LORD*. While, perhaps not referring to tattooing and body piercing as we know it today, we will see later that they developed from and are classified as scarification of which this verse is in reference to. Besides that, the point is that this type of marking of the body is a pagan, ungodly practice coming from heathen peoples. Some will argue that this is Old Testament law and quote the previous verse which forbids the cutting of beards to say if tattooing is wrong, so is the trimming of beards. First, it wasn't the trimming of beards, but the trimming of beards in mimic of the manner of the pagans. (Or at least a prohibition in order that God's people would look different from the pagans in the midst of whom they would dwell.) Something could be said here about dressing in the fashions of the world, or immodest dress that is being accepted by the world. Second, the verse following this says not to sell your daughter as a harlot. If the verse about beards invalidates what is said in the verse about markings on the body, then it also invalidates the verse about prostituting one's daughter. Although this doesn't pointedly address tattoos and body piercing as we know it, it does in principle address them. It came from pagan heathen practice (as we shall see) and it is an invading and altering of the body.

2. How does it hinder my relationship with God?
The very beginning of our relationship with God is separation from the world. *2 Cor 6:17.18 Wherefore come out from among them, and be ye separate, saith the Lord,*

and touch not the unclean thing; and I will receive you, and will be a Father unto you, and ye shall be my sons and daughters, saith the Lord Almighty. Also our prayer life will be affected if we are doing anything we know is contrary to what the Bible teaches. *Psa 66:18 If I regard iniquity in my heart, the Lord will not hear me*.

3. How will it effect, not only my testimony, but the image of Christ and our church to others?

Now let's turn to principles regarding tattoos and body piercing. Both identifies one with the world. 1. Tattoos are wrong for the Christian by reason of association. First, tattoos originated in unchristian, pagan societies around social and pagan religious practices. There is evidence of them first in Egypt in 2,000 BC. Historical Egypt is forever a symbol of the anti-God world. Later, tattooing is found in what is now New Zealand and China. In America, tattooing was first popular among sailors who had visited these foreign ports and received tattoos, many times while they were drunk, and imported them on their bodies back to America. Tattooing, until recently, has been most popular with the counter-culture youth (those rebelling against structure and authority), gangs, prison inmates, and some fashion models. Tattoos thus have been a symbol of the rebellious, criminal, tough guy types. Coming from pagan origins, adopted by anti-culture, anti-authority types, tattooing is simply not something that Christians should want any association with. 2. Body piercings were traditionally done only by the primitive tribes who didn't know the God of Israel. There are many examples recorded dealing with how pagans abused their bodies:

The false prophets of Baal *'cut themselves after their manner with knives and lancets, till the blood gushed out upon them,' 1 Kings 18:28*. In *Mark 5:5*, The demon-possessed man of Gadara cut himself with stones and ran around naked. It was the custom of the Ishmaelite <u>men</u> to wear gold earrings *(Judges 8:24)*. The character of Ishmael and his descendants is given in *Gen 16:12 And he will be a wild man; his hand will be against every man, and every man's hand against him; and he shall dwell in the presence of all his brethren*.

A. We are dealing with how tattoos and body piercing effects your testimony. It would seem that they mark you with the sin associated with those taking these marks of paganism. We are told in *1 Th 5:22 Abstain from all appearance of evil*. If one abstains from tattoos and body piercing, Dr. John Teague says: *"It will help you to be pleasing to God; it will help you to not fall into the category of being a hypocrite it will protect your witness for Christ; it will demonstrate your knowledge of the Word of God; it will verify your relationship to the true Vine. The true Vine will only produce fruit derived from that true Vine. It will not produce fruit that is not distinguishable from a different kind of vine; it will not put you in a compromised position that you may never recover from; it will help you render acceptable service to God; and it will keep you from the sin of disobedience."*

B. How do tattoos and body piercing affect the image of Christ in you? It tells us in *Gen 1:27 So God created man in his own image, in the image of God created he him*. It tells us in *Psa.139:14* that our bodies are a wonderful creation from the time we were conceived in our mother's womb. To altar our bodies by means of tattooing or body piercing is not accepting our bodies as God made them. Webster's definition of a tattoo is to *"puncture (the skin) with a needle and insert indelible colors so as to leave permanent marks or designs"*

C. How do tattoos and body piercing affect the image of our church to others?
We are living in a culture where the world and the church blend in together. In many churches in their youth activities they will do *'face paintings'* on the faces of young people, or give *'church tattoos'* for them to use. Is this not promoting the use of tattoos? How can it be anything else? The image of a church in a community is reflected by what that church practices and how people live their lives in the world

4. Am I willing to repent of it and seek God's power, rather than my own power to overcome it? It is to be understood that when one pierces their body, or has tattoos, unless they find some means to remove the tattoos or scars, they will carry them to their grave. So to repent of already having done it, will not remove the scars and imprints on your body. But there are Godly people who have repented and are sorry for having punctured, or pierced their body when they were living in sin, and the Lord has justified them through the shedding of His life's blood on Calvary.

Go to Dr. John Teague's website http://brotherteague.com/books.htm for an in-depth study on the subject of 'Tattoos and Body Piercings.'

Weights and Besetting Sins
Fact Sheet 2

A Profile Of The One Who
Helps To Make It Easy For You To Sin

*Heb 12:1 Wherefore seeing we also are compassed about
with so great a cloud of witnesses, let us lay aside every
weight, and the sin which doth so <u>easily</u> beset us, and let
us run with patience the race that is set before us,*
I have read this verse many times but there is one word that
has stood out as I have studied for this series of messages.
The word is **'easily'**. Webster defines easily--*in an easy
manner; with little or no difficulty, no discomfort*. If you do
not lay aside the **'weights and sins'** in your life you will be
easily beset by Satan. To help you better understand your
enemy here is a fact sheet using the same 4 basic questions.
*A profile is a short, vivid biographical and character sketch-
-Webster*

1. What does the Bible say about Satan?

The Bible says a lot about him. It tells us about his rebellion against God in *Ezek. 28:11-15* and *Isa. 14:12-15*. It gives a full account of his activities. He is described in a number of ways. Among them: **tempter**--We are all aware of his temptation of Jesus for 40 days in the wilderness, recorded in 3 of the 4 Gospels. However, we find in *1 Thess.3:5* that Paul was concerned about him tempting the believers. He was concerned enough to send Timothy; **liar**--He is the father and inspirer of lies *(John 8:44; Acts 5:3)*. We also see in *John 8:44* he is a **murderer and devourer**; he is intent on the destruction of God's people, as well as his destroying and devouring the lives of the unsaved. *(1 Pet.5:8)*; we also see here that he is our **enemy, or adversary**: he is relentlessly opposed to the children of God *(Mat.13:25)*; **accuser and slanderer**; his name, Devil, *'diabolos'*, means a person who throws things at people *(Rev.12:10)*; a **counterfeiter**, capable of presenting an innocent, even a religious 'front.' *(2 Cor.11;14,15)*; **hinderer**; He seeks to put things in the way of the Christian seeking to do God's will *(I Thess.2; 18)*; **misleader**, he uses his evil spirit to mislead in doctrine and causes apostasy *(I Tim.4:1)*;**trickster**, he uses subtle ways and means of confusing the Lord's people *(Eph.6:11; 2 Cor.11:3)*; **stimulator of lust**; normal desires are not wrong; but inflamed, uncontrolled sensuality is a tool of Satan *(Eph. 2:2,3)*; **ensnarer**: he is out to trap the Christian to sin so that his testimony will be ruined *(1 Tim.3:7; 2 Tim.2: 26)*; **deceiver**; by all possible means he seeks to create false impressions, innuendos, misunderstandings *(Rev.12:9; 2 Thes.2;9,10*. He is a **promoter of pride**; he stimulates man's high estimation of self *(Gen.3:5; I Tim.3:6)*; **oppressor**; he uses depression and discouragement as weapons to undermine the Christian's sense of purpose *(Acts 10:38)*. He sure worked on Elijah in *1 Kings 19* didn't he? **Troubler:** he seeks to invade the physical realm and limit the effectiveness of God's children *(2 Cor.12: 7)*; **blinder of men's minds**; His purpose is to keep men in ignorance of the light of the Gospel *(2 Cor.4:4; Eph.4:18,19)*; the **ruler of darkness**; his kingdom is totally without the light of truth, peace and love *(Acts 26:18; Col.1:13)*; **director of demon activity**, he controls an army of evil spirits *(Eph.6:12)*; **suppressor of the Word of God**: He constantly seeks to hinder the proclamation, acceptance and use of the Scriptures *(Mat 13:19a; 38,39)*; he is **God and prince of this world**; he foments 3 cravings described in *I John 2:16; John 12: 31)*; **creator of division**: he sows dissension between believers *(2 Cor.2: 10,11)*.

With all these descriptions of Satan we ought to be able to recognize the devil for who he is, and how he makes it *'an easy manner; with little or no difficulty*—to beset us in *'sins or weights'* we may have in our lives. Therefore we ought to **lay aside every weight, and the sin which doth so** **_easily_ beset us**.

2. How does he hinder my relationship with God?
He is the ruler of darkness in the world and it tells us in *Eph 6:12 For we wrestle not against flesh and blood, but against principalities, against powers, against the rulers of the darkness of this world, against spiritual wickedness in high places*. Any time the devil can get us to follow him in darkness, as we are beset by any weights or sins in our lives, our relationship [fellowship] with God is broken. As we're

easily beset by his deceit, we know our fellowship with God is broken. *1 John 1:6,7 If we say that we have fellowship with him, and walk in darkness, we lie, and do not the truth: but if we walk in the light, as he is in the light, we have fellowship one with another, and the blood of Jesus Christ his Son cleanseth us from all sin.* If you are a child of God—*Ye are all the children of light, and the children of the day: ye are not of the night, nor of darkness, 1 Th 5:5.* So we must not walk in the darkness of sin. Any sin, no matter how small you may think it is will hinder your relationship with God. If you are unsaved, the devil will hinder you any way he can from coming to the light. This is why as believers we must not hide the Gospel from them that are lost *(2 Cor.4:3)*, as the condition of unbelievers is given in the following verse, *In whom the god of this world hath blinded the minds of them which believe not, lest the light of the glorious gospel of Christ, who is the image of God, should shine unto them, 2 Cor 4:4*

3. How will he, the devil, affect not only <u>my testimony</u>, but the <u>image of Christ,</u> and <u>our church</u> to others?
Any time the devil gets you to sin, or do anything that is questionable in your life, he knows your personal testimony will be effected with those you come in contact with. Even if it is something that you may not think is all that bad, if it is questionable, do not do it. We are told in *1 Th 5:22 Abstain from all appearance of evil*. Some sins are often referred to as the *'grey areas'* of sin. If they are *'grey'* sins that means there is a tinge of darkness in them, and the devil wants to hurt your testimony.

The devil wants to mar the image of Christ in any way he can. And one of the ways he mars Christ's image is by a person who says they are a Christian and are walking in darkness. To be a *'Christian'* is to be Christ like. The devil no doubt laughs with glee when some person says they are a Christian and yet don't live like a believer in Christ. Unbelievers use hypocrites as an excuse for not coming to church.

The image of our church is displayed to those outside the church by the way we live our lives the *'other 6 days of the week.'* In some churches the devil has made the image of the church like the image of the world. People are told to *'come as they are and they leave as they were.'* The devil is using worldly churches to draw the crowds and the unsaved, [the world] interprets that as a successful ministry. Some of the mega churches you see on TV preach a God of forgiveness without any repentance.

4. Am I willing to repent and seek God's power, rather than my own power to overcome him?
The first thing you must do is repent of your sin—that means to turn from Satan and turn to Jesus seeking His forgiveness of any *'weights or sins'* the devil has easily beset you in. Don't ever forget our battle is ***against spiritual wickedness in high places***. The devil is more powerful than you, but God is all powerful and ***'greater is he that is in you, than he that is in the world,' 1 John 4:4***.

A graphic illustration of how the devil works is given at the website that gives an *'Interview With the Devil'* at http://www.InterviewWithTheDevil.com

Weights and Besetting Sins
Fact Sheet 3

What Is Wrong With Dressing Immodestly?

What is immodesty? is the question that must first be addressed before the facts of dressing immodestly is dealt with. To be modest Webster says: *behaving, dressing, speaking, etc in a way that is considered proper or decorous [good taste]; be decent.* So to be immodest is the opposite of that—*indecent* and Webster adds *'not shy or humble; to be bold; or forward.'* Even with Webster's definition we see that it is not proper, even for unbelievers, to dress immodestly. You would think people would not have to be told what is immodest. To dress immodestly is more than wearing shorts, halter tops, and skimpy swim suits, as you'll see in this fact sheet. Certainly shorts, halter tops, and skimpy swim suits are immodest, but there is much immodest dress in our day, i.e., tight-fitting jeans and slacks, low necklines, pants or skirts that have a low cut waste line hanging on the hips, open midriffs, short and slit skirts and dresses, and any tight fitting or thin clothing that reveals the secret parts of the body. This all applies to men and boys, as well as to women and girls.

1. What does the Bible say about it?
The Bible says anything that exposes the body indecently, or draws attention to the secret parts of the body, is the sin of immodesty. *In like manner also, that women adorn themselves in modest apparel, with shamefacedness and sobriety,1 Tim 2:9*. Webster's definition of *'modest'* parallels Strong's definition of the Greek word used here, it means *'orderly, i.e. decorous:--of good behavior'*. What is it that is to be modest? *Apparel*—clothing; garments; attire. I want you to notice the secondary definition Webster gives of immodesty: *'not shy or humble; to be bold; or forward.'* Does this not also fit with *1 Tim 2:9b*, *with shamefacedness and sobriety*? When one is *'not shy or humble; to be bold; or forward,'* then obviously there is no **shame-facedness and sobriety**. *1 Tim 2:10* continues to deal with one's apparel—*But (which becometh women professing godliness) with good works'*. I found in a previous study of the uni-sex attire of our day, the *'becometh'* here means that one is to stand out as a woman; not to stand out in the private parts of the body, but it means to stand out distinctively feminine. The punctuation marks were added in your English Bible, they were not in the original Greek text. After I looked at the meaning of the word *'becometh'* and I saw that the parentheses was added by the King James

translators and the other punctuation marks were added by translators—if I were a King James translator I would have punctuated the verse different. (Don't read in here that I am downgrading the KJV, I preach and teach from it and I always encourage other believers to.) The word *'array'* *(v.9)* which is clothing, also helped me to arrive as to how I would translate and punctuate to get what I believe it is saying. Here is how I would translate *v.10* and punctuate it—'*But array which becometh women,* (comma) *professing godliness with good works'*. Whether you agree with me or not, you can see what I believe the verse says even with the parentheses in there. The word *'becometh'* is *prepi*, from the root word *prepo*, which means *'to stand out, to be conspicuous, to be eminent, seemly, fitting.'* The verses tell you ladies that you are not only to dress modestly—keep your clothes on —but that you ought to stand out as a woman as well. You are to be conspicuous as a woman.

With believers there shouldn't be any disagreement when it comes to immodest dress. There are many Scriptures condemning immodesty (nakedness) throughout the Bible; too many Scriptures for anyone to have an argument for immodest dress, whether it is wearing shorts, mixed swimming, or any other activity where males or females dress immodestly. *Isa. 47:2-3* states very clearly that to **make bare the leg and uncover the thigh** is to uncover one's nakedness--**thy shame shall be seen**. Anyone who will make a thorough study of the word *'nakedness'* in the Bible will be convinced that it is a sin, other than in the husband and wife relationship. Immodest dress will cause the sin of adultery to be committed in the heart of man *(Matt 5:28)*.

The Bible says the sin of immodesty is also anything drawing attention to the secret parts of the body. In **Prov 7:8-10** we find a significant passage of Scripture telling us there is such a thing as **'the attire of an harlot'**; **v.22** tells us that the foolish **'go after her straightway'**. In **v.27** it says **Her house is the way to hell, going down to the chambers of death**. I don't have to go into great detail as to what it means when it says **'the attire of an harlot.'** If you have ever driven through the blue light districts of any large city, or as far as that goes, if you have watched TV that depicts the undercover policemen and policewomen in arresting those who are harlots, you have seen the *'attire'* they wear to identify with them and then make their arrest.

2. How does it hinder my relationship with God?

As was noted in *Fact Sheet #1 on 'tattoos and body piercing'*, the very beginning of our relationship with God is separation from the world. **2 Cor 6:17.18 Wherefore come out from among them, and be ye separate, saith the Lord, and touch not the unclean thing; and I will receive you, and will be a Father unto you, and ye shall be my sons and daughters, saith the Lord Almighty**. We're to be separate from the world in appearance, apparel and fashion if we are to have a relationship that is pleasing to God. Nakedness became a sin after the fall of Adam and Eve in the Garden of Eden. They **'sewed fig leaves together and made them aprons', Gen.3:7**, but they hid in the trees and there were no others around at that time to see them. Their appearance caused embarrassment and fear. It would be great if those who bare their bodies would take steps to get out of public view as they did. But they couldn't hide from God, as He knew where they were, though He said **v.9, Where are thou?** The fig leaf aprons were not sufficient covering for the Lord made *'coats of skins and clothed them,' v.21*. The moral law of God against nakedness was also given in the ceremonial law in the way they constructed their place of worship—*Exo 20:26 Neither shalt thou go up by steps unto mine altar, that thy nakedness be not discovered thereon*. Our relationship with the Lord will also be affected in how we approach Him in our place of worship, and in our daily living.

3. How will it effect, not only my testimony, but the image of Christ and our church to others? After sharing what I have about immodest dress, is it necessary for me to tell you that it will have an effect on your testimony, the image of Christ and our church to others? If you dress modestly, your clothes speak clearly to the world that you are one of God's children. But it involves more than just dressing modestly, as it says in *1 Tim 2:10, 'professing godliness with good works'* We are to *'present our bodies a living sacrifice unto God'* and in doing that we will not be *'conformed to this world, Rom.12:1,2.'* It is interesting that the word *'con-formed'* is the very same word translated *'fashioning'* in *1 Pet 1:14 As obedient children, not fashioning yourselves according to the former lusts in your ignorance*. If we fashion after [dress like] the world our testimony will be ruined.

4. Am I willing to repent of it and seek God's power, rather than my own power to overcome it? If your wardrobe is immodest, then you need to *'lay aside* [repent of] *that which doth so easily beset you* and start dressing modestly.

For a further study on modesty:
http://www.dtbm.org/message detail.asp?fileid=749. and
also the website:
http://www.seriousfaith.com/series_details.asp?seriesid=
34

Weights and Besetting Sins
Fact Sheet 4

What Is Wrong With Abortion?

1. What does the Bible say about it?

The Bible has much to say concerning God creating man and life beginning with our conception. *Gen 2:7 And the LORD God formed man of the dust of the ground, and breathed into his nostrils the breath of life; and man became a living soul. Job 33:4 The spirit of God hath made me, and the breath of the Almighty hath given me life. Job 10:8 Thine hands have made me and fashioned me together round about;. Job 31:15 Did not he that made me in the womb make him? and did not one fashion us in the womb? Psa 139:13-16 For thou hast possessed my reins: thou hast covered me in my mother's womb. I will praise thee; for I am fearfully and wonderfully made: marvelous are thy works; and that my soul knoweth right well. My substance was not hid from thee, when I was made in secret, and curiously wrought in the lowest parts of the earth. Thine eyes did see my substance, yet being unperfect; and in thy book all my members were written, which in continuance were fashioned, when as yet there was none of them.* All of these Scriptures and many more cited on the hand-out, *'Sanctity of Life Scriptures,'* shows us that it is a child that is conceived in the womb. John the Baptist is called a *'babe'* while he was still in the womb of his mother, Elizabeth. *Luke 1:41 And it came to pass, that, when Elisabeth heard the salutation of Mary, the babe leaped in her womb*.

Not only do we have Scriptures to show that life begins at conception, for now we have technology that wasn't available before and have learned a great deal since Roe v. Wade. The past 34 years have given us insight on what happens during those <u>nine months in the womb</u>. They have also given us more information on the <u>physical</u> and <u>psychological</u> dangers of abortion, and millions of women are still facing the after-effects. We have learned that both unborn babies and their mothers need help and protection. http://www.members.tripod.com/~joseromia/samuel.htm <u>l</u> is a web page that shows, while undergoing spina bifida surgery in utero, 21-week-old fetus Samuel Armas grips the finger of Dr. Joseph Bruner through the incision.

The Bible clearly says that we are not to take another person's life. *Gen 9:6 Who-so sheddeth man's blood, by man shall his blood be shed: for in the image of God made he man*. One of the Ten Commandments specifically says, *Thou shalt not kill, Exo 20:13*. One of the seven abominable sins in *Prov 6:i6*, is *'hands that shed innocent blood'*. Not only is the one who does the abortion guilty of this sin of '*shedding innocent blood,*' but those who allow it are guilty as well. It is not always the teenage girl that bears most of the guilt, for sometimes it is the boy who is the father of the child who insists that she get an abortion, and sad to say, grandparents of the unborn child will have their grandchild killed rather than bear the shame of an unwed child. I pray for the day when the abortion mills will be illegal and we will have some Godly, righteous judges that will carry out as it says in **Exo 21:22 If men strive, and hurt a woman with child, so that her fruit depart from her, and yet no mischief follow: he shall be surely punished, according as the woman's husband will lay upon him; and he shall pay as the judges determine**. It says of abortionists in **Deut. 27: 25 Cursed be he that taketh reward** [money] **to slay an innocent person**.

In the current issue of '*Integrity: A Journal of Christian Thought,*' printed by the Free Will Baptists Theological Commission, Mark R. Paschall writes an article on '*The Changing Landscape of the Abortion Debate.*' He writes of the barbaric procedure of partial birth abortion and says, "The legislation which protects the barbaric, violent act known as 'partial birth abortion' illustrates the consequences of accepting this argument based on women's rights. It should never cease to be a chilling experience for the Christian to hear a politician speak out in favor of partial birth abortion as we have recently witnessed. While most readers are probably aware of the level of depravity and Satan-induced blindness required to perform this act, its existence cannot be ignored in any discussion of the current state of the abortion debate. Partial birth abortion is known in the medical literature as

"intactdilation and extraction" (D & X), and a brief description makes this clear. After dilating the cervix for two days, the abortionist pulls the live infant, feet first, out of the womb. Carefully leaving the head inside the mother, because failure to do so would leave the doctor open to murder charges, he then punctures the base of the skull with scissors, inserts a hollow tube into the wound, and sucks out the baby's brain. This allows the largest part of the baby, the head and skull, to be crushed, and now the recently murdered child can be easily extracted from the mother and the corpse disposed of. As difficult as it is to believe, this procedure is the rallying cry of many politicians as they pander to any group which might boast their chances of election." A testimony of a nurse who witnessed it is given at:
http://www.cfra.info/43/testimony.asp

2. How does it hinder my relationship with God? This is a question dealt with in the other fact sheets on tattoos and body piercing, dressing immodestly, and the fact sheet on Satan, with *'sin which doth so easily beset us,' Heb.12:1*. Satan will use even small sins at times to beset us and keep us from *'running with patience the race that is set before us'*. But in my experience in counseling those who have had an abortion, I can say this sin is destructive in your relationship with God, as well as your relationship with those who are the closest to you. Many have repented of it—they will never do it again, but they have never asked the Lord for His forgiveness. Consequently they cannot pray like they should for they know it says in *Psa 66:18 If I regard iniquity in my heart, the Lord will not hear me*. They know what it says in *Isa 59:1-3a Behold, the Lord's hand is* *not shortened, that it cannot save; neither his ear heavy, that it cannot hear: but your iniquities have separated between you and your God, and your sins have hid his face from you, that he will not hear. For your hands are defiled with blood*. God in His mercy does continue to reach out with His hands and hear with His ears, to those who will not only repent of their sin, but ask God to forgive them, and to use them in helping others. Which leads to the next question in our fact sheets. .

3. How will it effect, not only my testimony, but the image of Christ and our church to others? God will mightily use those who have been delivered from sin and help others struggling with the same sin. This is why nouthetic counseling is effective, as a person who has been victorious in their faith can use the Bible more effectively in counseling some sin problems than the pastor, for he has never been where they have been. This can definitely have a positive effect of our church to those who need the help that can only come from God and His Word. It will be a testimony that our church is *'pro-life.'* How sad it is that some *'churches'* do not take a stand against the murder of the unborn.

For any who may have had an abortion, or know of someone who has, there is help for them on a website entitled *'After Abortion'*, the link
http://www.afterabortion.org/
One website that is very interesting gives the testimonies of some who are abortion survivors and now involved for pro-life. There are some heartbreaking experiences given on the website at http://joseromia.tripod.com/survivors.html

'Weights and Besetting Sins
Fact Sheet 5

What Is Wrong With The New Versions
Of The Bible?'

1. What does the Bible say about it? The Bible has much to say concerning the preservation of the original manuscripts, which are the inspired Scriptures. *Psa 12: 6,7 The words of the LORD are pure words: as silver tried in a furnace of earth, purified seven times. Thou shalt <u>keep</u> them, O LORD, thou shalt <u>preserve</u> them from this generation for ever.* The word translated *'keep'* here is *'shamar'* [shaw-mar]; Strong's says it means *to hedge about, i.e. guard; generally to protect, attend to, etc.:-- beware, be circumspect, take heed, keep, mark, look narrowly, observe, preserve, regard, reserve, save, sure, to watch as a watchman.* The word *'preserve'* here is the Hebrew word *'natsar'* [naw-tsar']. Strong's says it is *a prim.*

root; to guard, in a good sense (to protect, maintain, obey, etc.); to observe, preserve. What are we to keep and preserve? **The words of the LORD are pure words**, i.e., that is the inspired Word of God. **2 Tim 3:16 All scripture is given by inspiration of God, and is profitable for doctrine, for reproof, for correction, for instruction in righteousness**: Note it says **'all Scripture'** is inspired. The past generations have preserved the Word of God for us. It says of the Jews in **Rom 3:2. . Unto them were committed the oracles of God**. Oracles are utterances of God that they have passed on to us. This Gentile generation that we are living in is failing to preserve the words [utterances] of God for the coming generations, as through new versions we are distorting God's Word for the generations to come. We are to preserve all of the Bible, and not pervert it like the new versions [perversions] of the Bibles are doing. What does the word *'pervert'* mean? We usually think of Webster's definition: *'a perverted person; esp., a person who practices sexual perversion.* There is not only sexual perversion going on, but there is Scriptural perversion. Webster's defines this kind of perversion in the further definition he gives, which is, *to cause to turn from what is considered right, good, or true; to misdirect; lead astray; corrupt; to turn to an improper use; misuse; to change or misapply the meaning of; misinterpret; distort; twist; to bring into a worse condition; debase.*

The *New Greek Text of Westcott and Hort*, which these perversions of the Bible uses in their translations is *corruption, deletion, omission, addition, rejection and confusion.* The Bible says the following about adding to, or taking away from the Word of God and we better heed the warning and do what we can do about it.

Rev 22:18,19, For I testify unto every man that heareth the words of the prophecy of this book, If any man shall add unto these things, God shall add unto him the plagues that are written in this book: and if any man shall take away from the words of the book of this prophecy, God shall take away his part out of the book of life, and out of the holy city, and from the things which are written in this book.

Deu 4:2 Ye shall not add unto the word which I command you, neither shall ye diminish ought from it, that ye may keep the commandments of the LORD your God which I command you.

Deu 12:32 What thing soever I command you, observe to do it: thou shalt not add thereto, nor diminish from it.

Prov 30:5,6 Every word of God is pure: he is a shield unto them that put their trust in him. Add thou not unto his words, lest he reprove thee, and thou be found a liar.

Can the Scriptures be any plainer than these verses give us?

2. How does it hinder my relationship with God? Here is where the devil does his work, in hindering our relationship with God, as well as what is covered in the next question, our relations with others. It affects many of the doctrines of the Bible, as are given on the website at the end of this fact sheet. One of the doctrines they do great damage to is the preeminence of Christ. The devil wants preeminence as he did in his rebellion and fall in the beginning. He still wants to cast doubt on God's Word as he did with Eve in *Gen 3:1, Yea, hath God said*. The doctrine of the judgment of God for sin is another thing the new versions omit, as they delete 'hell' in many verses of their versions and the words **'damned', 'damnation'** are not even found in the NKJV, as they use the *New Greek Text of Westcott and Hort* for their translation, and not the KJV as their title implies Repentance of sin is another important doctrine they tamper with and remove in many places. The one verse they alter that promotes the *'once saved always saved'* doctrine is, ***Rom 8:1, There is therefore now no condemnation to them which are in Christ Jesus, who walk not after the flesh, but after the Spirit***. The NIV drops the last part of this verse and footnotes it, so that people get the wrong idea that they are *'in Christ'* and they do not have to worry about their being condemned as they continue in sin, but as you can see the promise is to those ***who walk not after the flesh, but after the Spirit***. My relationship with God will be hindered when I don't know what Bible to read that He may speak to me. Many new believers in our day are confused about the Bible to buy and read. It was not until all of the new translations that there was such confusion and people bought the KJV.

3. How will it effect, not only my testimony, but the image of Christ and our church to others? I have already said that it affects our doctrine. Earlier I noted ***2 Tim 3:16 All scripture is given by inspiration of God, and is profitable for <u>doctrine</u>, for reproof, for correction, for instruction in righteousness***: Doctrine it says in Strong's is *'instruction (the function or the information): doctrine, learning, teaching'* Webster defines it, *something taught; teachings; something taught as the principles or creed of a religion.* Our belief in doctrine will affect how we live, and our testimony will either portray the image of Christ to others, or we'll have no testimony. The Scriptures you will note also *reproves* us, *corrects* us, and *instructs* us in a life of righteousness. How sad it is to see those who claim the name *'Christian'* and it is very obvious they either do not know what the Bible says about righteous living, or they could care less what it says. Perverted Scripture will bring perverted doctrine, and this will bring a perverted lifestyle. Not in the sense of Webster's first definition above, but one's life will be like the perverted version one may be reading: *corrupt, deletion, omission, addition, rejection and confusion.*

This is the 5th Fact Sheet that I have prepared and I feel what is said and believed about the Bible in this one has a direct relation to the other topics I have covered, which were: tattoos and body piercing, a profile of the devil, immodesty in dress, and abortion. We must get back to the true Word of God and not reading and believing the Bibles that are not clear on the Lordship of Christ, repentance, and Godly living.

Open the following websites to learn more about the perversions of the Bible http://av1611.com/kjbp/articles/freeman-doctrines1.html is the website stating Bible Doctrines Affected by Modern versions http://www.jesus-is-savior.com/Bible/1611_authorized_king_james.htm is ' *The King James Bible Defended!'* website with numerous articles to read and audio files of messages to listen to.

http://av1611.com/kjbp/ is *The King James Bible* page with articles, charts and links http://www.av1611.org/niv.html is a website on the *'New International Perversion'*

Weights and Besetting Sins
Fact Sheet 6

What is Wrong With Cremation?

Cremation is disposal of the dead by reducing the body to ashes through a burning process. There are three basic questions that that I've used in the previous fact sheets, they are:

1. What does the Bible say about it?

2. How does it hinder my relationship with God?

3. How will it effect, not only my testimony, but the image of Christ and our church to others?

The message I am preaching is based on these facts, as I see them from the Bible.

1. What does the Bible say about it? There are two known cases of cremation in the Bible. In *Josh.7:25,26* it is used of Achan as a method of judgment of God, not the disposing of a body. In *1 Sam.31:8-13* again it is not used as a means of burial or disposing of a body but for special purposes to keep from further misuse of the body.

It was not a Hebrew or Scriptural custom. Over and over again in the Bible God com-mands the burning of things as a sign of displeasure and is a dishonorable way of disposing of a body. Throughout the Bible the destruction of a human body or of an object by fire is used as a sign of divine wrath. Some examples: Sodom and Gomorrah *(2 Pet. 2:6)*; Nadab and Abihu *(Lev.10:1,2)*. The men who rebelled with Korah *(Num.16:35)* The example of idols *(Exo.32:20; Deut. 7:25; 2 Kings 10:26; 1 Chron. 14:12)* The example of magic books *(Acts 19:18,19)*. The example of unsaved cast into the lake of fire for eternal punishment *(Rev.20:15)*. The cremation of children sacrificed to the false god of Baal was an abomination to God. *Deut.12:31, Thou shalt not do so unto the Lord thy God: for every abomination to the Lord, which he hateth, have they done unto their gods; for even their sons and their daughters they have burnt in the fire to their gods*. Archeologists have found huge numbers of urns of cremated ashes at the sites of the heathen worship of Baal. *Jer 32:35, And they built the high places of Baal, which are in the valley of the son of Hinnom, to cause their sons and daughters to pass through the fire unto Molech*.

As believers, Scripture tells us that our body is the *'temple of the Holy Ghost which is in you,' 1 Cor 6:19* and that our body, and our spirit are God's and we are to glorify God in them *(1 Cor 6:20)*, then it says in *Rom 14:8, For whether we live, we live unto the Lord; and whether we die, we die unto the Lord: whether we live therefore, or die, we are the Lord's.* It seems to me there is to be sanctity of the body from conception in the womb until that resurrection morning, *'in the which all that are in the graves shall hear his voice,' John 5:28*.

There are plenty of examples in the Bible, as well as in secular history, of God's people burying their dead, not cremating them: *Gen 15:15, And thou shalt go to thy fathers in peace; thou shalt be buried in a good old age*. Abraham buried Sarah *(Gen.23:19)* Abraham was buried *(Gen.25:9,10)* as well as Rachel, Leah, Isaac, Rebekah, Jacob, Miriam, Aaron, Joshua, Gideon, Samson, Samuel, David, Solomon, Elisha, and many others. Joseph was buried *(Gen 50:26)*. God buried Moses *(Deut.34:5,6)*. John the Baptist was buried *(Mat 14:10-12)*. Jesus was buried *(1 Cor.15:4)*. The word *'buried'* is used 106 times in Scripture.

Amos 2:1 is often used to support a prohibition against cremation: *Thus saith the LORD; For three transgressions of Moab, and for four, I will not turn away the punishment thereof; because he burned the bones of the king of Edom into lime*.

Cremation, while practiced in Biblical times, was not commonly practiced among Israelites. It was considered historically to be a 'pagan' practice.

2. How does it hinder my relationship with God? Some believe that the destruction of the body will hinder the bodily resurrection from the graves that will occur *(1 Cor 15:35-58; 1 Thes. 4:16)* which is hard to justify because you have a lot of bodies that are destroyed by fire against their will, i.e., early Christian martyrs. As well as, given enough time, each and every body decomposes to dust *(Gen. 3.19)*. Holding to the idea that 'a body must exist' limits God's power, tying His ability to the existence of a 'body'.

3. How will it effect, not only my testimony, but the image of Christ and our church to others? Cremation has a heathen origin and purpose. For instance, why do the Hindus and those of other heathen religions cremate? They do it in the belief that the dead are not raised again. The heathen practice cremation in the belief that the dead will be reincarnated. The silence of the Bible on reincarnation tells us that it is a heathen belief system. To practice this heathen custom would go against what the Bible says about copying the ways or customs of the heathen. We cannot copy a heathen custom that has no resemblance of biblical Christianity. In fact, when copying the heathen customs that go against God's clear revelation of truth, we are placing our stamp of approval upon them. The timeless principle that we must follow is this: We should not copy heathen customs that mock truth and Christianity. *Jer.10:2a* says, *Learn not the way of the heathen.*

It tells us in the Bible about the sacredness of our bodies, not only when we were being formed in the womb *(Psa.139:13-18)* but also while we live here on earth. *(1 Cor 6:19, 20)* If we believe this, then we will not desecrate our bodies in any way. We were created in the image of God- *Gen. 1:27*. I believe this image has to do with the physical, which is temporary while we exist on earth, as well as the spiritual fact that we are an eternal being and will exist forever. God came to earth in a fleshly body to redeem us from the curse of sin-*John 1:14 **And the Word was made flesh, and dwelt among us***. I believe our testimony will be hindered by not only how we treat our body while here on earth, but as well as to how we treat our body when life passes.

Your responsibility, even in death, is to honor God by sending the world a lasting testimony of your faith in God's resurrection program! Arrange your funeral plans ahead of time and be prepared to honor God's Word and the resurrection program of our Lord through burial. Practice burial, as God's people have always practiced, so that you might outwardly demonstrate your own faith as a Christian in God's resurrection program from our earthly temple. The Lord Jesus Christ was buried, and He is our great example (see *John 19:38-42*). In fact, we are told to follow His example in service *(John 13:15)* and suffering *(1 Pet. 2:21)*. Therefore, it is only fitting and right to follow His example in burial as we follow the steps of the Master. Just as the Lord Jesus Christ was buried in certainty that He would rise again on the third day according to the Scriptures *(1 Cor. 15:4)*, even so the Christian body is to be buried and await a future resurrection.

Attached are various statements on cremation; *'Cremation: What Does God Think?'* by David W. Cloud is a lengthy discussion; *'The Bible Presbyterian Church Statement on Cremation'* shows how they deal with it where it is a practice to cremate; *'What About Cremation'* by Kelly Sensenig is a 13 page discussion of cremation; *'What About*

Cremation' by Ronnie Williamson is a timely article on the subject; *'What Does The Bible Say About Cremation?'* by Garner Smith has five reasons for believers not to use cremation as a means for disposing of the body.

Section Three
Cantata

295295

One Day - Easter Cantata
Composed by Vernon Long

This Easter Cantata was broadcast on WWGM Radio in Nashville, TN and KJCF Radio in Festus, MO, while I was a student at the Free Will Baptist (Welch) College in Nashville, TN. I worked at the radio station and the following personnel at WWGM helped with narration in the cantata: Faye Lindsey, Roy Bee, Scott Marshall, and Bob Clark. The Music Department of Free Will Baptist Bible College did some of the musical arrangements for the cantata. Following is the introduction to the program:

Hello, this is Vernon Long inviting you to join us for the next two hours for our special Good Friday program. On the first part of the program we will be presenting the *'Seven Sayings of Christ From the Cross,'* and the second part of the program will be a cantata I composed a few years ago entitled, *'One Day'*. This is the third holiday special with *'My Friends of Nashville.'* Our last special program concerned the birth of our Lord and Saviour Jesus Christ and today's program concerns the reason for His incarnation, as He was born to die for the sins of mankind. The song, *'One Day,'* begins with His birth and then progresses through His sinless life and ends with His Second Coming.

The cantata was also presented at the Leadington Free Will Baptist Church in Leadington, MO, while I was pastor there by the very talented musicians of the church.

One Day - Easter Cantata
Open with singing "One Day" (Choir)

NARRATOR: In the beginning was the Word and the Word was with God, and the Word was God. And the Word was made flesh and dwelt among us, and we beheld His glory, the glory as of the only begotten of the Father, full of grace and truth. ("Redeeming Love" will be played as background music)

SONG: "Redeeming Love" (Solo)

NARRATOR: Jesus of Nazareth, a man approved of God among you by miracles and wonders and signs, which God did by Him in the midst of you, as ye yourselves also know. (Continue playing "Redeeming Love" in background)

SONG: "Jesus Loves Me" (Children)

NARRATOR: And many other signs truly did Jesus in the presence of his disciples, which are not written in this book; but these are written, that ye might have life through His Name. (Background music-"For God So Loved The World", then the youth choir hums this chorus as the narrator says:

NARRATOR: For God so loved the world, that He gave His only begotten Son, that whosoever believeth in Him should not perish, but have everlasting life.

SONG: "For God So Loved The World" (Youth Choir)

NARRATOR: Now the feast of unleavened bread drew nigh, which is called the Passover. And the chief priests and scribes sought how they might kill Him; for they feared the people. Then one of the twelve, called Judas Iscariot, went unto the chief priests, and said unto them, What will ye give me, and I will deliver Him unto you? And they covenanted with him for 30 pieces of silver. And from that time he sought opportunity to betray Him. (Thirty Pieces of Silver" as background music)

SONG: "Thirty Pieces of Silver" (Trio)

NARRATOR: Now before the feast of the Passover, when Jesus knew that His hour was come that He should depart out of this world unto the Father, having loved His own which were in the world, He loved them unto the end. And supper being ended, the devil having now put into the heart of Judas Iscariot, Simon's son, to betray Him; Jesus knowing that the Father had given all things into His hands, and that He was come from God, and went to God; He riseth from the supper, and laid aside His garments; and took a towel and girdeth Himself. After that He poureth water into a basin, and began to wash the disciple's feet, and to wipe them with the towel wherewith He was girded. After He had washed their feet, and had taken His garments, and was set down again, He said unto them, Know ye what I have done unto you? Ye call me Master and Lord: and ye say well; for so I am. If I then, your Lord and Master, have washed your feet; ye also ought to wash one another's feet. For I have given you an example, that ye should do as I have done unto you. When Jesus spake unto them the Great Commission, He said, Teach all nations to observe all things whatsoever I have commanded you. ("Emblems of Thy Condescension" as background music)

SONG: "Emblems of Thy Condescension" (Quartet)

NARRATOR: Jesus saith, I speak not of you all: I know whom I have chosen: but that the Scripture may be fulfilled, He that eateth bread with me hath lifted up his heel against me. He it is to whom I shall give a sop. And when He had dipped the sop, He gave it to Judas and Jesus said unto him, That thou doest, do quickly. Judas then having received the sop went immediately out: and it was night. Therefore, when he was gone out, Jesus said, Now is the Son of Man glorified, and God is glorified in Him. A new commandment I give unto you, That ye love one another: as I have loved you, that ye also love one another. Jesus lifted up His eyes to heaven and said, Father, the hour is come; glorify thy Son, that thy Son may also glorify thee; as thou hast given Him power over all flesh, that He should give eternal life to as many as thou hast given Him. And this is life eternal, that they might know Thee, the only true God, and Jesus Whom thou hast sent. I have glorified Thee on earth: I have finished the work thou gavest me to do. ("Tell Me the Story of Jesus" as background music)

SONG: "Tell Me the Story of Jesus" (Choir)

NARRATOR: Jesus saith, For I have given them the words that thou gavest me; and they have received them, and I have known surely that I came out from Thee, and they have believed that Thou didst send me. I pray for them for they are Thine, neither pray I for these alone, but for them also which shall believe on me through their word; that they all may be one, even as we are one, that they also may be one in us: that the world may believe that Thou hast sent me. (At this time start playing in the background, "Neath the Old Olive Tree.") When Jesus had spoken these words, He went forth with His disciples over the brook Cedron, where was a garden, and His disciples also followed Him. And when He was at the place, He withdrew Himself from Them about a stone's cast and kneeled down and prayed saying, Father, if Thou be willing, remove this cup from me: nevertheless, not my will, but Thine be done. And there appeared an angel unto Him from heaven, strengthening Him. And being in agony He prayed more earnestly: and sweat was as it were great drops of blood falling down to the ground.

SONG: "Neath the Old Olive Trees" (Solo)

NARRATOR: Judas, one of the twelve came and with him a great multitude with swords and staves, from the chief priests and elders of the people. Judas gave them a sign, saying, whomsoever I shall kiss that same is He: hold Him fast. And he came to Jesus and said, Hail Master; and kissed Him, then came they and laid hands on Jesus and took Him. One of them which was with Jesus stretched out his hand and drew his sword, and struck a servant of the high priest and smote off his ear. Then Jesus touched his ear and healed him and said, Put up again thy sword into its place: for all that take the sword shall perish with the sword. Thinkest thou that I cannot now pray to my Father, and He shall presently give me more than ten legions of angels?

SONG: "Ten Thousand Angels" (Solo)

NARRATOR: Now at the Feast of the Passover the governor was to release unto the people a prisoner, whom they would, and they had a notable prisoner, called Barabbas. Therefore, when they gathered together, Pilate said unto them, Whom will ye that I release unto you? Barabbas, or Jesus, which is called Christ? The chief priests and elders persuaded the multitude that they should ask Barabbas, and destroy Jesus. The governor said unto them, Whether of the twain will ye that I release unto you? They said, Barabbas. Pilate saith unto them, What shall I do then with Jesus which is called Christ? They all say unto him, Let Him be crucified! Then released he Barabbas unto them: and when he had scourged Jesus, he delivered Him to be crucified. Then the soldiers of the governor took Jesus into the common hall, and gathered unto Him the whole band of soldiers. And they stripped Him, and put on Him a scarlet robe. ("His Robe" as background music.)

SONG: "His Robe" (Trio, duet, or solo)

NARRATOR: And after they had mocked Him, they took the robe off from Him and put His own raiment on Him, and led Him away to crucify Him. And when they were come unto a place called Golgotha, that is to say, a place of the scull, they gave Him vinegar to drink mingled with gall: and when He had tasted thereof, He would not drink and they crucified Him. ("Blessed Redeemer" as background music)

SONG: "Blessed Redeemer" (Trio or quartet)

NARRATOR: And when the even was come, there came a rich man of Arimathea, named Joseph, who also himself was Jesus' disciple: he went to Pilate and begged the body of Jesus. Then Pilate commanded the body to be delivered. And when Joseph had taken the body, there came also Nicodemus, which at the first came to Jesus by night, and brought a mixture of myrrh and aloes, . About a hundred pound weight. Then they took the body of Jesus, and wound it in linen clothes with the spices, as the manner of the Jews is to bury, and they laid the body in Joseph's new tomb, which he had hewn out in the rock, and rolled a stone unto the door of the sepulcher and departed. Now the next day the chief priests and Pharisees came unto Pilate saying, Sir, we remember that that deceiver said while He was yet alive, After three days I will rise again. Command therefore that the sepulcher be made sure unto the third day, lest His disciples come by night and steal Him away and say unto the people, He is risen from the dead: so that the last error shall be worse than the first. Pilate said unto them, Ye have a watch: go your way, make it as sure as ye can. So they went, and made the sepulcher sure, sealing the stone, and setting a watch.

(At this time start playing in the background, "Christ Arose.")

Now upon the first day of the week, very early in the morning, they came unto the sepulcher and they found the stone rolled away and they entered in and found not the body of Jesus. And it came to pass as they were much perplexed thereabout, behold two men stood by them in shining garments, and as they were afraid and bowed down their faces to the earth, they said unto them, Why seek ye the living among the dead? He is not here, but is risen, remember how He spake unto you when He was yet in Galilee, saying, The Son of man must be delivered into the hands of sinful men, and be crucified, and on the third day rise again.

SONG: "Christ Arose" (Choir)

NARRATOR: He showed Himself alive after His passion by many infallible proofs, being seen of them forty days, and speaking things pertaining unto God. When they were therefore come together, they asked Him saying, Lord, will thou at this time restore again the kingdom of Israel? and He said unto them, It is not for you to know the times or the seasons, which the Father hath put in His own power. But ye shall receive power, after that the Holy Ghost is come upon you: and ye shall be witnesses unto me both in Jerusalem, and in all Judea, and in Samaria, and unto the uttermost part of the earth. (At this time start playing, "Jesus is Coming Again.) And when He had spoken these things, while they beheld, He was taken up; and a cloud received Him out of their sight. And while they looked steadfastly toward heaven as He went up, behold, two men stood by them in white apparel, which also said, Ye men of Galilee, why stand ye gazing up into heaven? This same Jesus, which is taken up from you into heaven, shall so come in like manner as ye have seen Him go into heaven.

SONG: "Jesus Is Coming Again" (Choir)

NARRATOR: And a voice came out of the throne saying, Praise our God, all ye His servants, and ye that fear Him both small and great.

SONG: "All Hail The Power of Jesus Name"

CLOSING SONG: "One Day" (All who participated in cantata singing)

Section Four
Information
Order blank

Message Series and Sampler Message
Number of Messages - In Each Series

Autobiography of a Faulty Foundation

Free Will Baptist Church Covenant: (5)
What FWB Believe About Giving Ourselves - I Thess.1:1-6

What Do Free Will Baptist Believe: (75)
The Intermediate State of Death – 1 Cor.15:35-38; 42-44

Seven Churches of Revelation: (16)
The Revelation of Jesus Christ - Rev 1:8, 11, 17b-20

Nehemiah Series: (12)
A Mind to Work – Neh.4:1-6

Sermon on the Mount: (55)
Is Fasting Scriptural? – Matt. 6:16-18

Ten Commandment Series: (20)
America and the 10 Commandments - Exo.20:3-17

First Thessalonians Series: (50)
The Sounds of His Coming - 1 Thess. 4:16

Divorce Messages: (5)
Biblical Grounds for Divorce - Matt.5:31,32; 1 Cor.7:10-15

Living by Faith Series: (41)
Seeking God is Essential - Heb.11:6

Acts of the Apostate Series: (20)
Acts of the Apostates – Jude 1-25

 Weights and Besetting Sins Series   (9)
What is Wrong With . . . ? – Heb.12:1,2
What is Wrong With Cremation? - 1 Cor 6:19,20; Heb.
12:1,2

Last Words of Christ From the Cross: (7)
Words of Anguish - Matt.27:32-46

Malachi Stewardship Series: (9)
Wherein Have We Robbed Thee? - Mal.3:8-12

First John Series: (37)
The Unpardonable Sin - 1 John 5:16,17; Mat 12:31,32

Warnings in Hebrews Series: (6)
The Danger of Willful Sin – Heb.10:26-31

Pigeon Forge Messages: (2)
The State of the Ship - Ezek 27:26
Is There Not Here a Prophet? - I Kings 22:4-8

ORDER BLANK FOR CDs

$12 each for slim case/$20 each for vinyl case, buy 2 and get 1 free

[ ] Monitor Messages	FREE	FREE
[ ] What Do Free Will Baptists Believe?	12.00	20.00
[ ] Messages on the Holy Spirit and Spiritual Gifts	12.00	20.00
[ ] Stewardship Messages and Promotions	12.00	20.00
[ ] Sanctity of Life	12.00	20.00
[ ] Sowing the Precious Seed	12.00	20.00
[ ] Holidays and Special Services	12.00	20.00
[ ] The Time is At Hand	12.00	20.00

Total Amount of Order _____ _____

Name _____   E-mail address_____

Address _____   Telephone _____

_____   Date ordered _____

Following are the contents on each of the Monitor Messages CDs:

The *'Monitor Messages'* CD contains manuscripts of 368 messages, 3 videos, 2 booklets, and fact sheets on tattoos and body piercing; Satan; immodest dress; abortion; new [per]versions of the Bible; and cremation.

The CD *'What Do Free Will Baptists Believe'* contains manuscripts of 80 messages on the Free Will Baptist Covenant and Treatise.

The CD *'The Holy Spirit and Spiritual Gifts'* contains manuscripts of 24 messages on the doctrine of the Holy Spirit and 13 messages on the Spiritual gifts.

The CD *'Stewardship Messages and Stewardship Promotions'* contains 102 manuscripts of stewardship messages, 11 stewardship promotions [with graphics] and messages used in the campaigns. There are also many other stewardship messages and graphic promotions I used at other churches.

The *'Sanctity of Life'* CD contains manuscripts of 12 messages concerning abortion, 57 articles on abortion, and 3 graphic videos of abortion.

The *'Sowing the Precious Seed'* CD contains messages and methods of soul winning evangelism; 3 videos, 1 booklet, and other helps in evangelism.

The *'Holidays and Special Services'* CD contains 532 manuscript messages and numerous articles on holidays and special services, 3 booklets and 6 videos. It is a resource especially for pastors and preachers.

The *'Time is At Hand'* CD contains 89 messages on death, and the end-times we are living in. The prophesy messages are not dogmatic, but will challenge you to further study of the end-times.

www.ingramcontent.com/pod-product-compliance
Lightning Source LLC
Chambersburg PA
CBHW061424040426
42450CB00007B/890